"Gary McIntosh is one of the leaders in research on growing churches and has made a tremendous contribution in this area. His latest book, *Growing God's Church*, explores a number of factors that contribute to growth. Anyone who is interested in knowing about growing churches should read this book. Everyone who is interested in actually working in a growing church needs to read this book."

—**Elmer L. Towns,** cofounder and vice president, Liberty University

"Dr. Gary McIntosh's in-depth research project and its practical findings on effective evangelism are a true gift to the kingdom. Every leader with a desire to fulfill the Great Commission should read *Growing God's Church* as soon as possible. The takeaways are revolutionary for the way we do outreach today. I will definitely be recommending this thoughtful, well-written book to all of my Coaching Networks."

—**Nelson Searcy**, lead pastor, The Journey Church, New York City, founder of www.ChurchLeaderInsights.com, and author of *The Renegade Pastor*

GROWING
GOD'S CHURCH

How People Are Actually Coming to Faith Today

GARY L. MCINTOSH

BakerBooks

a division of Baker Publishing Group
Grand Rapids, Michigan

© 2016 by Gary L. McIntosh

Published by Baker Books
a division of Baker Publishing Group
P.O. Box 6287, Grand Rapids, MI 49516-6287
www.bakerbooks.com

Printed in the United States of America

Library of Congress Cataloging-in-Publication Data
McIntosh, Gary, 1947–
    Growing God's church : how people are actually coming to faith today /
Gary L. McIntosh.
        pages cm
    Includes bibliographical references.
    ISBN 978-0-8010-1645-5 (pbk.)
    1. Church growth. 2. Evangelistic work. 3. Conversion—Christianity.
4. Church membership. I. Title.
BV652.25.M3158 2016
269'.2—dc23   2015024593

Scripture quotations are from the New American Standard Bible®, copyright © 1960, 1962, 1963, 1968, 1971, 1972, 1973, 1975, 1977, 1995 by The Lockman Foundation. Used by permission.

In keeping with biblical principles of creation stewardship, Baker Publishing Group advocates the responsible use of our natural resources. As a member of the Green Press Initiative, our company uses recycled paper when possible. The text paper of this book is composed in part of post-consumer waste.

16 17 18 19 20 21 22   7 6 5 4 3 2

To George G. Hunter III,
for his over fifty years of pioneering research
on how to effectively communicate
the gospel of salvation to secular people.

Contents

Acknowledgments

I wish to acknowledge several people or groups of people who made this research project a reality. First, my colleague and friend Michael Anthony, who assisted in the design and early analysis of the data. Second, the numerous pastors who distributed, collected, and returned surveys. Third, the nearly 1,100 persons who took time to complete each survey and share personal information about their coming to faith in Christ and a local church. Fourth, Carol McIntosh for entering the bulk of the raw information into a computer database. Fifth, Laura McIntosh and Gordon Penfold for reading and editing the early manuscript. Sixth, Mary Suggs and Mary Wenger for the final editing and oversight, which brought this project to publication. And seventh, to the late Win Arn for his belief in me as a speaker and writer. To all of these, I say "Thank you!"

Part 1

The Church Today

An Old Story Retold

It is an old story that has been told many times before, but like many good stories, it warrants telling once again. Sometime in about the year 30 of the Christian era, a man was sitting at his work when he encountered a person who was about to change his life forever. Matthew, who also went by the name Levi, had painstakingly worked his way up to be the primary tax collector in the area of Capernaum, located in Palestine close to the Sea of Galilee. Matthew worked for the Roman government authorities, but he had grown up in the area and knew the local people and customs well.

The people of Galilee were not wealthy, and the tax revenue that Matthew collected for Herod Antipas was a heavy burden on them. The fact that Matthew added an extra fee to the taxes to provide for his own salary left a bitter taste in the mouths of the people, and most saw him as a traitor to his own people. Indeed, the people of Galilee refused to be friends with Matthew, and so he spent a great deal of time with other tax collectors.

Little did people know, because he never spoke of it, that Matthew felt a deep loneliness and did not like being hated by his own community. Like most people, Matthew wanted to enjoy love and respect from his neighbors and family. Deep in his heart, he longed for a life of meaning. Being a tax gatherer had made him wealthy, he lived in a beautiful home, and his family owned every material item they desired. Still, he was not happy. He longed for inner peace that the great wealth he had amassed could not provide. Most of all, he wanted to be accepted by the people.

Being an educated man, and with his tax booth located in a central place, he easily observed the impact the new teacher was having on the people of Galilee. He had met Jesus once or twice and was surprised to find that Jesus did not criticize or curse him for being a tax collector. Every time Jesus engaged him in conversation, he did so in a respectful and loving manner. Matthew was drawn to Jesus but was cautious, not wanting to open up to just any stranger who came along. The years of abuse he had suffered from the people of Galilee made him cynical about ever having friends, but quietly he hoped that someday he would be accepted and loved.

The new teacher had caught his attention, particularly due to the merciful way he dealt with the most marginalized people in the community. One day Matthew observed Jesus when a man with leprosy came and knelt before him. Most religious teachers of the day screamed out, telling lepers to get away from them because they did not want to make themselves impure. To Matthew's astonishment, though,

Jesus healed the man of his leprosy. A few days later, Matthew heard talk about how Jesus had healed a centurion's servant who lived in Capernaum simply by declaring that the servant was free of disease. He also heard it whispered that Jesus had healed the fisherman Peter's mother by simply touching her hand. What was most astonishing was when Matthew saw Jesus drive demons out of people with just his spoken word. These and other actions by Jesus were discussed all over town, and Matthew was beginning to believe that perhaps Jesus had the answers he was seeking.

Then one day as Matthew was seated at his booth collecting taxes, Jesus walked by, stopped for just a moment, looked Matthew squarely in the eyes, and said, "Follow me." It was a crazy request. How could he leave his work at a moment's notice and simply follow this itinerant preacher? Before he knew it, though, Matthew found himself standing up, walking away from his table, and moving in Jesus's direction. It was really an outrageous thing to do.

Peter had done a similar thing, but Peter could always go back to being a fisherman if it did not work out with Jesus. Matthew, on the other hand, would never be able to go back to being a tax collector. He could never return to his booth. Surely he would suffer the ridicule of the people who already detested him. However, there was something about Jesus's call on his life. Matthew knew deep inside that his life had been changed simply because he had accepted Jesus's invitation to follow.

Before long Matthew realized something had changed. He was no longer the same man. He had lost his desire for money and material possessions. New thoughts were coming into his mind, and strangely, he began to think about the tax gatherers with whom he had often partied, traveled, and visited. He knew that many of them were struggling with acceptance, just as much as he had been until he found Jesus. What could he do to help them meet the man who had changed his life? He decided to invite Jesus and his friends to the evening meal at his home.

The evening meal was the largest and most important meal of the day. Matthew knew that many of his friends would be willing to come, if not to meet Jesus, at least to have a good meal together. But would Jesus come? Religious leaders in Galilee were loath to eat with tax gatherers and impure sinners who did not follow the regulations of the law. Eating together was an important social and religious testimony, as well as an indication of who was accepted and not accepted as friends. Nevertheless, if Jesus were to come, his willingness to dine with them would imply a willingness to accept the people that others rejected. After much thought, Matthew approached Jesus with the invitation and was excited when Jesus graciously accepted. He was truly wiser and more merciful than the scribes and Pharisees, and because of Matthew's invitation, many of his associates dined with Jesus that day.

A Perplexing Problem

Dining with Jesus is a metaphor for engaging our family, friends, and associates with the gospel of salvation. Since the death, burial, resurrection, and ascension of Jesus Christ, his followers have worked diligently to reach those outside of the church with the saving message of salvation. Yet over the last couple of decades, I have noticed the emergence of a perplexing problem among Christian churches. Simply stated, while churches are becoming more missional in their thinking, they are becoming less evangelistic in their practice; that is, they are less involved in helping new people dine with Jesus.

I realize that some observers of the North American church may disagree with me, but it is my perception that direct evangelism receives little emphasis, encouragement, or training in our churches. This is quite different from what I encountered in my early years of church ministry after I first placed my personal faith in Jesus Christ. Allow me to briefly share my story as an illustration of how evangelism was emphasized in past years.

> *While churches are becoming more missional in their thinking, they are becoming less evangelistic in their practice.*

I grew up in a nominally Christian home. My mother and grandmother had committed their lives to Jesus Christ during the Great Depression of the 1930s, were baptized, and, in their own words, "attended church every time the doors of the church were open." Unfortunately, life for both of them had taken several unexpected turns by the time I came along, and they drifted away from church, never to attend on a regular basis again.

Being good "Christian" people, they raised me to respect God and the Bible and to be a good boy, which meant no cussing. The need for me to personally decide to follow Christ, however, was never part of the conversation. Beyond a basic respect for God, my family, and the Bible, the only biblical education I received came through some early Christian television preachers and attendance at a two-week vacation Bible school one summer before I entered third grade, where I memorized the Ten Commandments and the Twenty-third Psalm.

My commitment to Christ came through the invitation of a friend who lived next door. Neil (his real name) was attending a small Bible church three blocks from our homes, and he regularly asked me to go to Sunday school—for three years! When he invited me to go with him, I always agreed to, but every time he came by on Sunday morning to pick me up, he found me asleep. Even today I hear echoes of my grandmother answering the door and saying, "I'm sorry, Neil, Gary's in bed, but you keep asking him, and one of these days he'll go with you." Grandmothers are, of course, always right, and one day I did get up and go with Neil to church, where I placed my faith in Christ alone for salvation. I started attending church, getting involved in ministry, and growing in my faith.

Soon I discovered that the church cared deeply about lost people. The gospel of salvation was preached regularly from the pulpit. Organizations like Youth for Christ, the Navigators, and the Billy Graham Association were esteemed as models of outreach, along with several mission organizations. Almost immediately after becoming a believer in Christ, I was instructed in how to share my faith and was encouraged to do so. Along with others from the church, I attended a Sunday school convention held in Denver, where the course options included several classes on evangelism of children and adults.

At Youth for Christ I was taught to counsel other students. I joined teams distributing Christian literature at local events and caught a vision for reaching friends in high school. In college I learned the "Four Spiritual Laws," canvassed neighborhoods, and visited other college campuses to share my faith.

Later, after graduating from seminary, I attended an evangelism conference that taught Evangelism Explosion

(EE), offering a new approach to reaching people. More than fifteen hundred people attended that conference to learn a more effective way to share the gospel. In those years EE was widely known, and I encountered numerous churches using it wherever I traveled.

On entering the pastorate, the first ministry I started was an evangelism training class. We called on visitors to share the gospel and went door-to-door in the neighborhood around the church facility sharing our faith. Following nine years of pastoring a local church, I spent several years leading friendship evangelism training conferences as part of the team at the Institute for American Church Growth. By my calculations, our team led about 225 events in a little over a decade, training some twenty-five thousand people to share their faith throughout the United States.

Until approximately 1995 every church at which I spoke, led training, or consulted gave evidence of a passion to reach people for Christ. Unfortunately, since the mid-1990s, the interest in evangelism has declined, except for a few denominations and local churches. For example, between 1983 and 1995, I conducted 115 training seminars for local churches and denominations, with nearly half (56) focused on evangelism. However, between 1995 and 2013, I have conducted 153 training conferences with only 1 focused specifically on evangelism!

My story illustrates the central place that evangelism held in church ministry just a few years ago. It is quite different today. There is less emphasis on evangelism in our churches than there used to be just two decades ago. Some will point out that the context in the United States has changed greatly over the last half century, particularly during the last twenty years; and indeed, it has changed greatly. The world in which we live and minister does not seem as open to hearing about

Jesus Christ and the gospel of salvation. The general culture has marginalized churches and Christians to the point that the classic gospel message is not respected or allowed an unbiased hearing. It is well established that we live in a post-Christian culture where it is much more difficult to speak about the Christian faith, sin, judgment, reconciliation, and the uniqueness of Jesus Christ as the only way to heaven. Christians in general are afraid to use the word *evangelism*, as it recalls memories of judgmental people, forced presentations, talking to strangers, and unwise practices of proselytizing persons against their will.

Generally Christians recoil at the thought of evangelizing their family, friends, and neighbors for fear of being labeled intolerant of other people's faith and lifestyles. It is my educated guess that at least 90 percent of churches and Christians are reluctant to proclaim the classic gospel of salvation, even on Easter Sunday. In place of evangelism, churches have adopted a concept of missional outreach, which usually means they do acts of love, mercy, and justice in their communities. Any sort of outreach that affects our communities and families for Christ is good, but it is equally important in today's postmodern society for Christians and churches to proclaim the Good News of salvation in Jesus Christ. Good works and deeds do open doors for sharing the gospel, but it is only the message of Jesus Christ's death, burial, and resurrection that has saving power.

Evangelistic Insights

This is the reason I am writing this book. While it is important in today's postmodern society for Christians to let their light shine through missional acts of service, it is equally important, perhaps more so, to proclaim the Good News of salvation in Jesus Christ. Individuals who receive a cup of cold water in the name of Jesus may think more highly of the church that dispenses the water, but they will still be eternally separated from Christ unless they believe in Jesus for salvation. Thus it is a central premise of this book that for churches and Christians to be truly missional, evangelism must be restored to a primary place in life and ministry. While there is certainly resistance to the gospel message in our current culture, the resistance to evangelism is more often in the church than in the world. Hurting people are still looking for direction and hope, which only the Good News of salvation in Jesus Christ can provide.

Closely related to this purpose—that we need to proclaim the Good News of salvation—is the reality that few leaders understand how men and women are finding faith or connecting with a church in today's world. Most church leaders continue to rely on old statistics that, while factual three to four decades ago, are no longer valid. For example, in the 1980s it was reported that 85 to 90 percent of people were coming to Christ through family and friends. This statistic is still widely quoted, but my research reveals it is no longer factual. Family and friends now account for just 59 percent of faith conversions, which is a decline by one-third in the influence of family and friends on evangelism. Another example reveals that thirty years ago pastors were responsible for just 6 percent of faith decisions, but my new research reveals that pastors and other staff members are now responsible for 17 percent

> *If a church desires to be truly missional, evangelism must be restored to a primary place in its ministry.*

of all commitments to Christ, which is a 283 percent increase in the impact that pastors are having evangelistically. While my new research reveals some changes in the manner people are coming to faith, it also confirms some old truths. For instance, it has long been believed that most churches reach people within a twenty-mile radius of the church's campus, usually referred to as a ministry area. My study confirms this belief, as 100 percent of new believers say they travel less than twenty miles to their church. Thus *Growing God's Church* will, as English novelist William Thackeray wrote, "make new things familiar and familiar things new."

Design of the Study

Although the topics of evangelism and assimilation have always been intertwined, serious research on how people come to faith in Christ and into his church is a recent endeavor. The well-known researcher and speaker Win Arn conducted the most influential study in North America during 1979 and 1980, and for more than three decades, his findings have continued to impact local church strategies for winning people to faith in Christ and connecting people to a church. While serving as vice president of consulting services for Arn's Institute of American Church Growth in the years 1983–86, I was active in communicating his original study to numerous churches. From my perspective, few studies over the last half century have had such major influence on church ministry as Arn's study. However, in the late 1990s, I began to notice that some of Arn's findings did not ring true in the numerous churches for which I was consulting. It occurred to me that it might be wise to rework Arn's original study to see how people were coming to faith in Christ and his church at the beginning of the twenty-first century.

Phase One—Preliminary Research

To assess my observations, I conducted a small preliminary study of eleven churches for which I had consulted and had statistical information. This exploratory study, "How People Come to Christ and the Church: A Case Study," was presented on November 12, 1999, at the annual meeting of the American Society for Church Growth, Indianapolis, Indiana. It confirmed my suspicion that things had changed since Arn's original study. Participants who listened to the presentation offered numerous suggestions and encouragement to move forward with a full-scale study.

Phase Two—Data Collection

Since my desire was to conduct a national study that would have validity across numerous denominations throughout the United States, I asked my colleague Michael Anthony from Talbot School of Theology, Biola University, to assist in the overall research design, development of a survey instrument, collection of data, and initial data analysis. Michael has a double PhD and is a recognized expert on research and survey design. Together we developed a list of potential questions and tested a preliminary survey before settling on the final instrument (see the appendix for a copy of the final survey used in this study).

We determined to survey only people who had joined a church within the two years before completing our survey. To locate new church members, we asked randomly selected pastors to distribute the surveys for us to people who had become part of their church within the previous two years. We began the process of distributing surveys to pastors in 2006 with the hope of compiling a minimum of 1,000 completed ones by 2008. The extra steps of having pastors distribute, collect, and return surveys from people in their churches ended up taking longer than we expected. However, by November 2008 we had collected enough surveys to do an initial data analysis, which Michael presented at the American Society for Church Growth annual meeting on November 14, 2008, in La Mirada, California. Once again, the questions and suggestions from participants provided helpful ideas for further analysis. Several pastors who were present at the meeting volunteered to help distribute additional surveys so we could reach our minimum of 1,000. By 2010 we had collected 1,093 usable surveys, entered the data, and were ready to complete our final analysis.

Phase Three—Analysis and Writing

After entering all of the survey information into a database, another of my colleagues, Kevin E. Lawson, EdD, who directs Talbot's PhD and EdD programs in education, assisted in cleaning up the raw information and running the preliminary data analysis. This was completed in 2013, but final analysis and writing the results was delayed until summer 2014 due to other projects on my calendar.

Altogether the study encompassed a span of six years for data collection and another four years for analysis and writing. In the final total, 1,093 surveys were received, representing twenty-seven denominations from forty-three different states. Validity is determined to be within +/– 4 points.

Respondents came from several traditions, such as Baptist (38.3 percent), nondenominational (23.6 percent), Wesleyan

(15.6 percent), Free Church (6.5 percent), Christian Church (6.2 percent), and Reformed (5.4 percent). The completed surveys represented 436 men (40.4 percent) and 641 women (59.5 percent). As for generations, 20 percent were Builders, 37 percent Baby Boomers, 40 percent GenXers, and 6 percent Millennials. Regarding location, 16.5 percent resided in rural areas, 13 percent in small towns, 33.5 percent in small cities, 24 percent in medium cities, 7 percent in large cities, and 6 percent in metropolitan cities.

Layout of the Book

Growing God's Church is organized around ten crucial questions—five biblical and five practical. Chapters 2 through 6 engage some of the biblical issues surrounding evangelism, namely: What is our mission? What is our priority in mission? What is our role in mission? What is the focus of our mission? And what is the context of our mission? As you may be aware, such questions are not new, but *Growing God's Church* calls us back to the classic biblical understanding of these issues.

The second part of this book reveals the findings from the study of how people are coming to Christ and a church. Chapters 7 through 11 ask and answer the following key questions:

Who led you to faith in Christ?
What method most influenced your decision for Christ?
Why did you begin to attend church?
Why do you remain at your church?
What is the pastor's role in evangelism?

The book closes with two chapters noting principles for effective evangelism and practical ideas you may begin to use immediately to increase your church's fruitfulness in evangelism by helping more people dine with Jesus.

If you could see more people come to faith in Christ through your church's ministry, would you be interested? If help were offered for connecting more people in your church, would you be interested? If more people in your church could understand, grasp, and enjoy evangelism, would you be interested? Then read this book. The answers are here, discovered from people who recently received Christ and connected with a church.

2

What Is Our Mission?

Jesus was wiser and more merciful than the scribes and Pharisees. He was on a mission to earth—a mission from his Father—and nothing was going to stand in the way of his accomplishing it.

What was his mission? Like many areas of life, the mission of Jesus had several aspects. His overall mission, what we might call his doxological mission,[1] was to glorify God the Father. The apostle John records the story of Jesus teaching in the temple during the Feast of Booths. The Jews who heard him speak were amazed, wondering how he could know so much when he had no formal education. Jesus replied to them, "My teaching is not Mine, but His who sent me. . . . He who speaks from himself seeks his own glory; but He who is seeking the glory of the One who sent Him, He is true, and there is no unrighteousness in Him" (John 7:17–18).

Jesus was seeking the glory of the one who had sent him on a mission that he completed, as he later declared, "I glorified You on the earth, having accomplished the work which You have given Me to do" (17:4). Jesus's principle mission was doxological, but how did this happen? How did Jesus bring glory to God the Father? Look again at his prayer, for he tells us exactly what he did. "I glorified You on the earth, *having accomplished the work which You have given Me to do*" (emphasis added). Accomplishing his earthly mission brought ultimate glory to the Father.

Jesus's Earthly Mission

I say Jesus's mission was an *earthly* mission, since it is clear that as part of the Godhead Jesus had a broad-based mission that included (and includes) the creating and sustaining of the world. The apostle John opened his Gospel with words that spoke about Jesus's mission as Creator: "In the beginning was the Word, and the Word was with God, and the Word was God. He was in the beginning with God. All things came into being by Him, and apart from Him nothing came into being that has come into being" (John 1:1–3). John went back to the beginning of creation to let us know that Jesus is God himself. As the Word, Jesus was not only with God but was God (v. 1), a construction in language meaning Jesus is of the same essence or being as God the Father. As God, Jesus had many missions or goals, some of which are revealed to us, and very likely many that are not. Who knows the mind of God but God himself (Rom. 11:33)?[2]

As part of the Godhead, Jesus had many missions, but his earthly mission was to "give eternal life" to all mankind

(John 17:2). This was his destiny, and Jesus referred to it throughout the Gospel of John as his *hour*. Jesus first mentioned it when talking with his mother, Mary, at a wedding in Cana of Galilee (2:1–11). In reply to Mary's request for him to make more wine, Jesus answered, "My hour has not yet come" (v. 4). At first one might think Jesus was simply saying that the time for making the wine was not at hand, but as one reads further through John's Gospel, it becomes evident that he meant much more. When walking in Galilee to attend the Feast of Booths, Jesus told his brothers, "My time is not at hand" and "My time has not yet fully come" (see 7:6, 8). Later John wrote twice: "His hour had not yet come" (7:30; 8:20). The repetition of the idea of Jesus's hour not at hand gradually increases tension as the reader, and no doubt the hearers, of Jesus's words wonder when his hour will come.

The anticipated announcement came on Palm Sunday after Jesus rode into Jerusalem on a donkey. Some Greeks told Philip they wished to see Jesus. Philip referred the request to Andrew, after which they both went to Jesus to tell him about the Greeks' request. Jesus answered, "The hour has come for the Son of Man to be glorified" (12:23). After all of the suspense, Jesus's hour had arrived. While Philip and Andrew did not fully understand at the time, Jesus was speaking plainly about his death. The next verse makes it obvious: "Truly, truly, I say to you, unless a grain of wheat falls into the earth and dies, it remains alone; but if it dies, it bears much fruit" (v. 24). By this analogy, Jesus referred to the fact that he must lose his life so others would gain eternal life. It was this act of dying over which he struggled as the Son of Man. He asked the Father to save him from this hour, but he finally declared, "*For this purpose I came to this hour"* (v. 27, emphasis added). It was the hour of his death, his crucifixion for all mankind. It was his hour "to be glorified" (v. 23). His death was not a time of tragedy but one of triumph! It was his earthly work! His earthly mission was to die on the cross as a sin offering for men and women, boys and girls.

This was the mission that God the Father sent Jesus to accomplish on earth. After Jesus asked the Father to glorify his name, a voice came out of heaven saying, "I have both glorified it, and will glorify it again" (v. 28), which was the Father's response. In this context, the Father must be referring to the cross. God the Father was glorified at the cross. Then Jesus confirmed that "the ruler of this world will be cast out" (v. 31), which was a reference to Satan's defeat through Christ's death on the cross (14:30; 16:11; Heb. 2:14–15; Rev. 12:10). Then Jesus emphatically declared that when he is lifted up, he "will draw all men to Myself" (John 12:32). The apostle John always used the idea of *lifting up* to mean Jesus on the cross (see John 3:14; 8:28; 12:32, 34). In the popular mind of the time, dying on a cross was degrading rather than exalting, but Jesus dramatically grasped the crowd's attention by turning the cross into a triumph of exaltation.

> *The earthly mission of Jesus was to die on the cross so that all whom God the Father had given him might have eternal life.*

As usual, the people who heard Jesus speak did not understand him. They expected him to take the position of an earthly king, but he spoke about his death. After they questioned him regarding this, Jesus called attention to the need to believe. "For a little while longer the Light is among you" (12:35). "While you have the Light, believe in the Light, so that you may become sons of Light" (v. 36). With this metaphor, he drew attention to his earthly mission again, but this time he identified himself as the Light.

In the beginning of his Gospel, John moved quickly from noting Jesus's mission as Creator (1:3) to focusing on his mission as Messiah. "In Him was life, and the life was the Light of men" (v. 4) is a continuing theme through the Gospel. Jesus was called both the "life" and the "light" of men, and the two are connected throughout the Gospel.[3] In his mission as Creator, Jesus gave the universe life and light (Gen. 1:1–2:3). John the Baptist came as a witness to the true Light (John 1:6–9). Jesus came as Light into the world that he made, but few recognized him. "But as many as received Him [the true Light], to them He gave the right to become children of God, even to those who believe in His name, who were born, not of blood nor of the will of the flesh nor of the will of man, but of God" (vv. 12–13).

Following the incident with the woman who was caught in adultery, Jesus declared, "I am the Light of the world; he who follows Me will not walk in the darkness, but will have the *Light of life*" (8:12, emphasis added). Light and life are again connected; to have one is to have the other. To have either, one must believe. "I have come as Light into the world, so that everyone who believes in Me will not remain in darkness" (12:46). John mentioned that he recorded certain signs or miracles, which the disciples observed with their own eyes, for this purpose: "that you may believe that Jesus is the Christ, the Son of God; and that believing you may have life in His name" (20:31). All of this was connected when Jesus said his hour had come. His earthly mission was simply to

31

die on the cross so that all whom God the Father had given him might have eternal life. As Jesus affirmed, "For this is the will of My Father, that everyone who beholds the Son and believes in Him will have eternal life" (6:40). Jesus was obedient to his earthly mission, and he sent forth a witnessing band of believers to spread the news that he was the Light and Life of the world and to call the peoples of the world to believe on him to receive eternal life.

A Witnessing Band

Our mission is inseparably bound with the mission of Jesus Christ. Throughout the Gospel of John, Jesus asserted he was on a mission from the Father. At least twelve different times in John's Gospel, Jesus declared that God sent him. For example, after talking with the woman at the well in Samaria, Jesus told his disciples, "My food is to do the will of Him *who sent Me* and to accomplish His work" (John 4:34, emphasis added). Later he healed a lame man by the pool of Bethesda and was criticized by the Jews for healing on the Sabbath. Shortly after this, the Jews sought to kill him, not simply because of his healing on the Sabbath, but because he claimed that God was his own Father (5:1–18). In the conversation that followed, Jesus instructed the Jews, "I can do nothing on My own initiative. As I hear, I judge; and My judgment is just, because I do not seek My own will, but the will of Him *who sent Me*" (v. 30, emphasis added). His very works bore witness that the Father sent him (vv. 36–37; see also 6:29, 38, 44, 57; 8:16, 18; 12:49; 14:24). God the Father sent Jesus and now Jesus transfers his mission to his followers: "As the Father has sent Me, I also send you" (20:21).

The sending of the disciples as a missionary band has theological roots. While none of the disciples were present at Jesus's birth, they engaged with him early in his earthly life. Looking back, John remembered, "The Word became flesh, and dwelt among us, and we saw His glory, glory as of the only begotten from the Father, full of grace and truth" (1:14). Some of them came to see Jesus as the "Lamb of God," a theological understanding (v. 36), and they followed Jesus, stayed with him for a short while (vv. 37–39), and invited others to share in their experience (vv. 41–46). From the beginning, the small fellowship of disciples was a missionary band witnessing to their experience with Jesus. What held them together was their theological understanding of Jesus following the initial testimony of John the Baptist. They were much more than a loving fellowship; they were a witnessing band of believers!

The power for witnessing came from the indwelling of the Holy Spirit. Jesus promised the small band of believers that he would not leave them alone after his resurrection but would send the Spirit. The Spirit bore witness at Jesus's baptism (vv. 32–34), Jesus spoke about the importance of the Spirit in conversion (3:5, 8), and he promised the Spirit would be with them after his resurrection (7:37–39; 14:16–26; 15:26–27; 16:13). Following his commission of the disciples— "as the Father has sent Me, I also send you"—Jesus breathed on them and said, "Receive the Holy Spirit" (20:21–22). Thus the Gospel of John concludes with the small band of disciples going forward as a witness in the power of the Holy Spirit. No longer are they a group of individuals but a sent group on a mission for Jesus Christ. Jesus pointed out the fact that they were a community on a mission when he said, "I also send you," using the plural form of *you* rather than the singular.

The disciples were sent not just as individuals but also as a group, a point Jesus repeated following his resurrection (v. 21). Jesus used the same approach his Father had used, and the earthly mission of Jesus was passed on to the small band of disciples whom he sent on a mission that eventually expanded to become a missionary church.

To what mission were the disciples sent? The mission of the disciples flowed out of Jesus's mission. Since the earthly work of Jesus was to bring eternal life to lost humanity, this is the continuing mission of his witnessing band of believers, now the church. The work is stated in terms of "eternal life," as Jesus communicated to Nicodemus in John 3:16–17. "God did not send the Son into the world to judge the world, but that the world might be saved through Him." The church's mission is to witness to the fact that eternal life is found only in Jesus Christ who died on the cross to pay for humanity's sin. This is highlighted in the seven "I am" allegories: "I am the bread of life" (6:35–48); "I am the Light of the world" (8:12; 9:5); "I am the door" (10:7–9); "I am the good shepherd" (10:11); "I am the resurrection and the life" (11:25); "I am the way, and the truth, and the life" (14:6); "I am the vine" (15:5).

The world of John's day was filled with numerous religions, each with its own understanding of how to have a relationship with the divine. The mission of the disciples, as well as ours, was to proclaim an exclusive way to the Father. Jesus shocked his hearers by declaring, "No one comes to the Father but through Me" (14:6). It is a message that has never been popular (certainly not in our day), but it is the message that must be proclaimed by the church. It was a message that the apostle John carefully constructed from chapter 1 onward. "No one has seen God at any time," John wrote; "the only begotten God who is in the bosom of the Father, He has explained Him" (1:18). "God so loved the world, that He gave His only begotten Son, that whoever believes in Him shall not perish, but have eternal life" (3:16). It is a message of an exclusive way to the Father, to eternal life, which must be delivered to the world.

It is also a message that calls for a verdict. Throughout the Gospel of John, a series of contrasts were laid out that naturally demand a decision. There is contrast between darkness and light, receiving and not receiving, faithlessness and believing, death and life, condemnation and salvation, wrath and eternal life. The tensions created by these contrasting concepts demand a response. People choose darkness or light, to believe or not to believe, wrath or life. One either rejects Jesus or accepts him; there is no middle ground (3:15–18; 12:48–49; 13:20; 20:26–29). Jesus "came to His own, and those who were His own did not receive Him. But as many as received Him, to them He gave the right to become children of God, even to those who believe in His name" (1:11–12).

The gospel message requires a verdict. One either rejects Jesus or believes in him; there is no middle ground.

The world is in rebellion against God, his Son, and his people. The disciples are "not of the world, even as I [Jesus] am not of the world" (17:16). Surely the world hates Jesus and his people (7:7, 18–19), so it is an enigma that the world is also the context where the mission of Jesus and his church is carried out. The world is winnable (3:16–19; 6:33, 51), and Jesus has sent his people "into the world" (17:18). While Jesus was not of the world, he never isolated himself from it. Rather, he engaged with the poor, the needy, the ignored, and even its leaders, both religious and political. As the mission of Jesus was carried out in the world, so the mission of the church must be carried out here.

What is our mission? It is to proclaim that eternal life is available to those who believe in Jesus Christ, particularly in his death on the cross, his burial, and his resurrection. It is to proclaim that Jesus is the unique Savior of the world and he is the only way to the Father, the only way to eternal life. As this chapter has illustrated, the apostle John viewed the mission of the church through a narrow lens of salvation. Is it too narrow? Is not the mission of the church larger than just preaching the Good News of salvation to a lost world? What about caring for the poor, feeding the hungry, and releasing the oppressed? Are these and other social challenges not part of the church's mission? If they are, what priority level do we assign to them in our daily practice? It is to these questions we turn in chapter 3.

Probing Questions

1. What was the earthly mission of Jesus Christ?
2. How did the original apostles understand the mission of Jesus Christ?
3. In what ways is the mission of the local church a continuation of the mission of Jesus Christ?

3

What Is Our Priority?

No one had heard from Jesus for nearly two months. The last time anyone could remember seeing him was at the Jordan River where he was baptized by John, who was known as the Baptizer, the son of Zacharias. A rumor was circulating around Galilee that something powerful had taken place when Jesus came up out of the water after being baptized. Some observers reported that God had spoken from heaven, declaring Jesus to be his Son. Others could not say exactly what happened, only that there was a noise in the air, perhaps just the wind. All agreed that Jesus was missing. What they did not know, could not have known at the time, was that Jesus went into the nearby wilderness, led by the Holy Spirit's urging, where he was tested for forty days by the devil (Luke 4:1–13).

Then as quickly as he disappeared, he was back. The people of Nazareth, where Jesus had been raised, heard he was traveling around the region of Galilee, teaching in synagogues to great acclaim. The word in the marketplace and the country roundabout was astonishing: Jesus was teaching with great power and authority like no one had heard or seen before. Naturally people in Nazareth wanted to hear Jesus teach too. Could it really be true that Joseph's son was now a great teacher? The idea of a great teacher of the Law coming from their town thrilled the people, but some, maybe most, harbored doubts that it could be true. If only he would come to Nazareth, they could see and hear him and judge for themselves.

The day finally came when they could all find out the truth about what they were hearing. Jesus entered Nazareth, and, as his custom was, he went into the synagogue on the Sabbath day, taking his place to read. The scroll of the prophet Isaiah was given to him, and he opened it and read, "The Spirit of the LORD is upon Me, because He anointed Me to preach the gospel to the poor. He has sent Me to proclaim release to the captives, and recovery of sight to the blind, to set free those who are oppressed, to proclaim the favorable year of the LORD" (vv. 18–19).

All eyes followed him as he rolled the scroll, handed it back to its attendant, and then sat down to teach. He announced, "Today this Scripture has been fulfilled in your hearing" (v. 21). At first these words pleased those in the synagogue, but as he continued to teach, his words shocked them—even angered them. In their rage they took him to the edge of the hill on which Nazareth was built, intending to throw him to his death, but Jesus quietly walked through the crowd and went on his way.

Jesus was on a mission—a mission that would lead him to the cross to die for the sins of the world—and nothing was going to stop him until he achieved it. However, the beginning of his public ministry in Luke 4:14–22 appears to indicate that he had other priorities, that of caring for the poor, the captives, the blind, and the oppressed—priorities that the church must also embrace. The church's very nature, like that of Jesus, is missional. Its missionary nature flows from the heart of the triune Godhead (Father, Son, and Holy Spirit). Since the church is the body of Christ, it must of necessity focus on mission. Indeed, any church (or group of churches) that is not involved in God's mission is disobedient. But where are we to place our priorities of time, energy, and money? Are we to give priority to evangelism or to social justice?

What exactly is our missional priority? One perspective suggests that the priority of the church is to be viewed *holistically*, including such things as taking care of the environment, contending for social justice, declaring God's reign, as well as preaching salvation through Jesus Christ. This view is often called the *Missio Dei* and suggests that since God is one, he has only one mission, rather than many missions, in the world. The church (and churches) must be about God's full or entire mission in the world and function equally in multiple arenas of ministry without giving priority to one area or another. Thus a church that is engaged in food distribution or counseling the jobless or cleaning the streets in its neighborhood is seen as just as involved in mission as a church that is engaged in church planting or preaching the gospel of salvation or baptizing new converts. As one writer puts it, "All that the church does in living its life and in carrying out its ministry is missionary by intent."[1]

This view sees churches that place a priority on evangelism and church planting as reductionist; that is, they reduce the whole gospel to just one small component. In this holistic view, witnessing and evangelizing are inviting others into the community of faith to participate in the reign of God in whatever form mission activity takes.

A contrasting view suggests that the priority of the church is to be viewed atomistically because it includes numerous objectives or tasks that are interrelated but not of the same priority. Thus while there are many good things that a church can and should do in this world, God has assigned a priority to the church for reaching the lost. The church, of course, as the *koinonia*, or community of faith, is to be involved in caring for the homeless, serving the disadvantaged, and meeting needs of those in distress, but these activities are Christian duties that all believers do in their regular course of life. Such activities are not the missional priority of the church. Witnessing and evangelizing are inviting the lost to become disciples through personal faith in the resurrected Christ. Or to put it another way, the priority of the church is to win the lost, baptize new believers, and teach everyone to obey what Christ taught.

While serving the common good, *the early church placed a priority on the greater good, that of saving souls.*

These two contrasting views have undergone and are undergoing a shifting theological emphasis in churches. Whereas evangelicals used to give priority to evangelism, many now contend that the church must balance social action with evangelism. It is suggested that by focusing on holistic ministry, the divorce between the sacred and the secular—the Great Commandment and the Great Commission—can be ended. Echoing ecumenical declarations of past generations, some evangelicals now are attempting to integrate the Great Commandment and the Great Commission—loving others and making disciples—as a holistic message. There is no priority in God's mission, just holism, some contend.

Christians have always embraced social justice. Throughout the thrilling history of the expansion of the Christian church, "an impressive means of attracting converts was the extensive humanitarian activity of the Church."[2] From the first, the church cared for its own poor (Acts 2:45; 4:34); then, as the church was able, it started orphanages, hospitals, hospices, and houses for widows and indigents. These, it must be admitted, were all started out of love but also as a means for preaching the gospel of salvation. While serving the *common good*, the early church placed a priority on the *greater good*, that of saving souls.

What are we to make of these two views? Is there a priority for church ministry, or are all ministries of equal value? In other words, when Jesus taught from the prophet Isaiah in the synagogue in Nazareth, did he institute a focus on justice versus a focus on salvation? Was he establishing a foundation for holistic church ministry or declaring something entirely different—perhaps a ministry that placed a priority on preaching the gospel of salvation?

A Salvation Theme

The Gospel of Luke sets forth a historical account of what took place surrounding the life of Jesus Christ. Luke used a *salvation theme* in developing his history, which came from the Old Testament prophet Isaiah. "How lovely on the mountains are the feet of him who brings good news" (52:7).[3] Throughout his Gospel, Luke incorporated the phrase "glad tidings" or "good news" as its central guiding message. This is evident in the five "songs" or "hymns" he compiled to begin his book, all of which tie the salvation motif into the person and work of Jesus Christ.

Luke began with the song of Elizabeth (1:42–45), which was prophetic testimony to John the Baptist and Jesus. As she declared Mary to be the mother of "my Lord," Elizabeth said, "the baby leaped in my womb for joy" (vv. 43–44). The central focus was on Mary's Magnificat. The Song of Mary was primarily one of salvation, as she stated, "My soul exalts the Lord, and my spirit has rejoiced in God my Savior" (vv. 46–47). It promised hope for the oppressed (v. 52), food for the hungry (v. 53), and faith in the promises of God for all who fear him (vv. 51–52, 54–55). After Elizabeth's son was born and named John, Zacharias praised God for accomplishing "redemption for His people" and raising up "a horn of salvation . . . in the house of David" (vv. 68–69). John was declared to be "the prophet of the Most High" who would prepare the way of the Lord (v. 76) and who would "give to His people the knowledge of salvation by the forgiveness of their sins" (v. 77).

The songs of Elizabeth, Mary, and Zacharias are all anticipatory and prophetic, but the song of the angels and the song of Simeon are both songs of praise for the fulfillment of God's promises. As the shepherds watched their sheep one night, an angel appeared, saying, "I bring you good news of great joy." The message was for Israel and "for all the people" (2:10). Then a choir of angels appeared and said, "Glory to

God in the highest, and on earth peace among men with whom He is pleased" (v. 14). It was a song of salvation, but "the theological implication of this song is that the offer of peace is open to all but requires an appropriate attitude of acceptance."[4] After a time of purification for Mary and for Jesus's circumcision, Jesus was taken to the temple where Simeon, a man full of God's Spirit, confirmed that Jesus was the Savior: "For my eyes have seen Your salvation, which You have prepared in the presence of all peoples" (vv. 30–31).

All of these five songs demonstrate the salvation motif of Luke. It is a salvation that reaches beyond Israel to all peoples. Salvation shines on all those who sit in darkness and the shadow of death (1:79). It is good news for all the people (2:10). It is a light of revelation to the Gentiles (v. 32). When Luke traced the lineage of Jesus, he did so all the way back to Adam (3:38), and this connected Jesus to all humans.

No one realized it at the time, but when Jesus disappeared for a short while, he was facing the challenges of the devil. Satan knew that Jesus had come to bring salvation to the nations (24:46–48) and tried to stop him by offering him the kingdoms of the world (4:5–7). Jesus resisted the devil's temptations and then inaugurated his mission at Nazareth in terms of the salvation theme to preach the gospel (v. 18).

In using Isaiah 61:1–2 Jesus declared three important things. First, his earthly ministry to bring salvation to all peoples had started. Jesus certainly was not the type of messiah they were seeking, and after listening to him for a short while, the people angrily rejected him and his message. The concepts of poor, captive, blind, and oppressed were no doubt taken literally by those who heard Jesus teach in the synagogue that day in Nazareth, but a shift occurred that they missed. Evidently Jesus was not speaking of the economically poor, those in actual prisons, or physically blind, or politically oppressed (none of these people were present in the synagogue). Rather, he was speaking of the spiritually poor, blind, captive, and oppressed.[5] His preaching was not good news to those listening to him that day because they were not the pious poor, that is, those who humbly knew their need for God. But for those who were poor in the spiritual sense, the good news of Jesus's death, burial, and resurrection was (and remains) good news.

The second important declaration Jesus made was that he was the anticipated Messiah who was bringing salvation with all of its hope for the spiritually sick, the poor, and the oppressed. This was clear in his response when John the Baptist sent two disciples to ask, "Are you the Expected One, or do we look for someone else?" (Luke 7:20). In response, Jesus told them to report to John, "*The* BLIND RECEIVE SIGHT, *the* lame walk, *the* lepers are cleansed, and *the* deaf hear, *the* dead are raised up, *the* POOR HAVE THE GOSPEL PREACHED TO THEM" (v. 22). No doubt, John the Baptist understood that Jesus was claiming to be the Messiah, for God had prophesied in Isaiah that Messiah would be "a light to the nations," would "open blind eyes," and bring "those who dwell in darkness from the prison" (Isa. 42:6–7). After Jesus left Nazareth, Luke reported that Jesus was healing and casting out demons—proof that he was the Christ (Luke 4:31–44). Thus the purpose of God bringing Jesus the Messiah into the world was to provide salvation for all peoples, including the Gentiles. It was truly

To preach the kingdom of God adequately is to issue a call to conversion.

the mission of the triune Godhead, as Luke demonstrated. God the Father, the Son, and the Holy Spirit were all involved in the bringing of salvation to the world through the incarnation.

Third, the activity of Jesus involved preaching. Three times in Luke 4:18–19, the Holy Spirit is said to have anointed Jesus to preach and proclaim. Later Jesus states that he "must preach the kingdom of God to the other cities also," for he was sent for that purpose (v. 43). Whatever "preach the kingdom of God" means, "to preach it adequately is to issue a call to conversion."[6] As Luke points out, preaching the Good News of salvation was the number one priority for Jesus and the disciples whom he sent out.

Three Sendings

Building on the salvation theme, Luke provided three reports of Jesus sending his followers out to preach. The salvation theme demanded that the followers of Jesus Christ go out preaching the Good News to all people, and the stories found in Luke are prophetic of the future church. Before his death and resurrection, Jesus sent out the Twelve and the Seventy. After setting the stage for his public ministry in chapter 4, Jesus continued to heal, teach, and gather a group of followers from whom he selected his close band of disciples. By chapter 9 the twelve disciples were a genuine band but still not completely aware of his full message and mission when Jesus called them together, gave them power and authority over demons and diseases, and sent them out to preach the kingdom of God (vv. 1–2). Even though they were not mature theologically or experientially, they had been with Jesus, knew some of his teaching, and had seen him minister to others, so they had some knowledge of what to do, and Jesus gave them further instructions. They were to travel light, with little organized structure (v. 3), and employ the principle of receptivity (vv. 4–5) or "acceptance and rejection"[7] by focusing on those receptive to their message. Their mission was to be one of harvesting rather than sowing and cultivating, and as such, they were not to waste time preaching the Good News to those who were unresponsive. With their limited knowledge and instructions, the Twelve went out and then returned to debrief their experiences with Jesus (vv. 6, 10–11). How Jesus's training method is to be understood and employed in church ministry today is open to different interpretations, but it demonstrates the missional nature of Luke's salvation motif. Jesus did not wait until the disciples were mature before sending them out. Rather, he sent them to proclaim what they knew and then used their successes and failures as teaching moments to instruct them in deeper understanding of his message.

Before Jesus sent his disciples on their second mission, he allowed them to experience several maturing episodes. These included the feeding of the five thousand (vv. 12–17), Peter's confession (vv. 18–21), instruction on the cost of discipleship (vv. 23–26), his transfiguration (vv. 27–36), personal failure (vv. 37–42), their need of humility (vv. 46–48), and awareness of his coming death (vv. 22, 44–45). By the time he was ready to send them on a second mission, they had matured greatly. This time Jesus expanded the mission to include seventy people. Again his mission was presented as one of harvest rather than sowing and cultivating, for the "harvest is plentiful, but the laborers are few" (10:2). It was a dangerous mission; they would be like lambs among wolves and were to maintain a mobile ministry (vv. 3–4). However,

Luke developed a "theology of option and verdict."[8] When people are presented with an opportunity for belief and they reject it, they will face a day of judgment.

On this second mission, the disciples learned much about power for witness and service. When the Seventy returned, they rejoiced in their fruitfulness (vv. 17–24), as they had power even over the demons. Jesus affirmed that he had given them power over power, that is, they had power with authority over the powers of Satan (v. 19). Jesus warned them not to be proud but to rejoice in their own salvation.

The salvation motif that Luke first presented in the account of the miraculous conception and birth of Jesus was quickly narrowed down to a final sending in chapter 24. Along the way, Luke imparted a great deal of information leading to the happenings of the Last Supper, the night in Gethsemane, the cross, and the thrilling resurrection before getting to his account of the final sending out of the disciples. Two important passages that concern our discussion of mission priority are found in chapters 15 and 19. The first includes the three stories of the lost sheep, the lost coin, and the lost son. All three stories stress the importance of finding what is lost. The story of the lost sheep centers on the joy in heaven over one lost sinner who repents (15:7). The story of the lost coin concludes with the assertion that even the angels in heaven rejoice over one sinner who repents (v. 10). The story of the lost son shares the joy of the father in finding his lost child (vv. 22–32). All three stories gently focus attention on the importance of finding lost people, an idea that Jesus later explicitly stated in the story of Zaccheus (19:10). The encounter of Jesus with Zaccheus ended in his belief and salvation (v. 9), after which Jesus stated his missional priority, "For the Son of Man has come to seek and

to save that which was lost" (v. 10).⁹ This clear statement of
Jesus, coming directly after the story of Zaccheus's belief
and salvation, can have only one meaning. The priority of
Jesus was to save lost people! The context allows for no other
interpretation.

Jesus's postresurrection sending follows his appearances
to and final teaching of his disciples. While the disciples experienced the living Christ by talking, touching, and seeing
him in the flesh (he even ate in their presence), Jesus taught
them from the Old Testament prophets (24:25–27, 44–46). By
aligning himself with the prophets of old, Jesus demonstrated that his missional priority had to be understood in the light of his death and resurrection, since they were the fulfillment of prophecy. At this point, Luke tied the final sending
of the disciples to the salvation motif of his entire account.
The priority of the disciples was to proclaim the Good News
to all the nations. What was the Good News? It was nothing
more or less than that forgiveness of sins following repentance was available through the death and resurrection of
Jesus Christ (vv. 46–48). The disciples had observed these
happenings and were sent on a mission to tell (witness) what
they had seen.

In the first two sendings Luke mentions, the disciples had
just part of the story, part of the message, and part of the
picture. As they were sent on their third mission, they had
the whole story, although more was to come, mainly the
coming of the Holy Spirit (v. 49). The small band of believers was to become the church whose missional priority was,

> *The priority of Jesus was to seek and save the lost.*

and is, to proclaim the Good News of salvation to all the nations (peoples) of the world, beginning at Jerusalem and then moving outward in concentric circles until reaching the ends of the world (v. 47; Acts 1:8). This was the priority of the church. This is our priority today!

Our priority to proclaim the gospel of salvation to all the nations does not mean we should ignore serving our communities or mankind. Service without proclamation and proclamation without service are both futile. It is the gospel preached *and* lived that impacts humanity and society with power. Both need to be preserved, and the church must practice both. In truth it is difficult, perhaps impossible, to disentangle preaching and service. Preaching the gospel of salvation must be done *among* the people, not just *to* the people. Yet it must also be admitted that the best service the church can render to humanity is the proclamation of the gospel of salvation. Numerous nonprofit organizations, Christian and non-Christian, address social justice issues around the world.[10] But only the church is called to proclaim salvation in Jesus Christ.

What makes the church unique is not its good deeds but its message of salvation in Jesus Christ. If we feed the hungry today but fail to preach the gospel of salvation and thereby see few or none turning to Christ, those we feed will ultimately die in their sins. They may be well fed, but they will go into eternity apart from Christ. The ultimate service is to win souls, whereby they go into eternity as children of God. Christ told his followers they were witnesses of this life, death, and resurrection. No doubt, there were hungry people in Galilee, and indeed in all of the places where they would preach the Good News, but he recognized that we must not ignore the incredibly ready for the incredibly needy. Other organizations can care for the poor, clothe the naked, and feed the hungry. Only the church (and churches) can proclaim the Good News of salvation in Jesus Christ. Goodwill Industries will not proclaim Christ crucified, buried, and risen. Neither will The Y (no longer the Young Men's Christian Association!) nor any government assistance program. Even among Christian ministries, observation demonstrates that where social service is prioritized over evangelism, very little evangelism actually occurs, a fact gradually being recognized by church leaders.

The most precious service we can render to our non-Christian neighbors and friends is to help them come to faith in Jesus Christ, who alone is the way to eternal life. Our commission is to go lovingly, yes, to go caringly, yes, and to go with healing, yes. Most important, however, is to go sharing the gospel of salvation made possible through the death, burial, and resurrection of Jesus Christ. This is our priority.

Probing Questions

1. Describe the differences between the priority of mission understood holistically and atomistically.
2. When Jesus said he was anointed to preach the gospel to the poor, what did he mean?
3. What is the church's priority regarding mission?

What Is Our Role?

Soon after Jesus had finished teaching in the synagogue at Nazareth, he continued throughout Galilee. Beside the Sea of Galilee, he encountered Simon and Andrew casting fishing nets into the water and called out to them, "Follow Me, and I will make you become fishers of men," after which they immediately "left their nets and followed Him" (Mark 1:17–18). Just a short distance away, he saw James and John, the sons of Zebedee, and challenged them to join him, after which they quickly left their work and followed along too.

When they all arrived at the synagogue in Capernaum, Jesus found a man who had an unclean spirit. The unclean spirit recognized Jesus as the Holy One of God and said so in a loud voice. Jesus rebuked the unclean spirit and commanded him to hold his peace and to come out of the man. The unclean spirit cried out once more with a loud voice and came out of the man. The people observed the interaction of Jesus, the man, and the unclean spirit curiously. They wondered if he was preaching a new doctrine and asked by what authority he commanded the spirits. Yet even as questions formed in their minds, they spread his fame throughout all the region of Galilee.

Action and Power

In gathering his disciples,[1] Jesus commonly called people from their workday world, for instance, fishermen and tax collectors, and then demanded loyalty and commitment from each one. He particularly called people who were self-starters, men of action, and not afraid of work. Once they had joined with him, he instructed them, experienced life with them, and in time, as they learned to participate in his mission, they became fishers of men (Mark 1:17; 3:14–19). The call of Christ came not just at one level of life but at many levels. He called people to become his followers, to place themselves under his tutorship to learn from him, and finally, to participate in his mission. Christ's call was, and is, always a call to responsibility, a call to action, a call to service!

The Gospel of Mark begins with the declaration that Jesus Christ is the divine Son of God (1:1). Throughout the book, though, Mark presented Jesus as a servant with the power to accomplish a mission for God. He was a man of deeds more than mere words, a man of action more than speculation, a man of power more than weakness.[2] "The Gospel of Mark pictures Christ in action. There is a minimum of discourse and a maximum of deed."[3]

Jesus came with Good News, which was to be believed (v. 15). He presented a verdict theology whereby one must choose either to repent, confess, and receive remission of sins or reject salvation and suffer the consequences. Selecting salvation often involves going through a period of unrest, a time of repentance, a moment of belief, a new mental state of peace, and a readiness to embrace a cross.[4] Jesus's gospel is worth sacrifice (10:29) and must be proclaimed to all the nations (13:10). The whole world was highlighted when Jesus declared that the house of God is "a house of prayer for all the nations" (11:17) and that the gospel will be preached to all the nations (14:9).

In the Gospel of Mark, Christ's mission is seen as a twofold program. In short, Jesus came with a gospel of salvation and of power. First, his mission is one of proclaiming salvation (1:14–38; 2:2). Jesus expected his followers to take action, for his powerful gospel was to be preached to the whole world. As an example that the gospel message was for all peoples, on the day of Jesus's crucifixion, the Roman officer, a Gentile, confessed, "Truly this man was the Son of God!" (15:39). Jesus's commission to his disciples was, "Go into all the world and preach the gospel to all creation" (16:15). True,

Christ's call is always a call to responsibility, a call to action, a call to service!

Jesus began in his own community with people from his own nation, but he gradually expanded his mission until he died for the whole world and rose in power. He commissioned his disciples to take the gospel everywhere beyond the confines of their own land. The sum of their message and missionary activity was to go into all the world and preach the gospel and to do it with power—the power that God in Jesus Christ provided (16:15–18).

Second, Jesus's mission is one of power. He preached a gospel of power that directly confronted the worship of all other gods. Jesus cast out demons and healed diseases to demonstrate that his mission came not just in words but also in powerful deeds from God the Father (healing—1:30–31, 34, 40–43; 2:3–5, 10–11; 5:22–24, 41–42; 10:46, 52; deliverance from demons—1:23–27, 34, 39; 3:11–12; 5:2–20), and Jesus sent his disciples out with the same power (3:13–15; 16:15–18). Without a doubt, the Lord demanded action from his followers and provided the power for their success.

God's Fellow Workers

Mark presents our role as servants of Christ preaching the Good News of salvation and persuading men and women, boys and girls to place their faith in Jesus Christ alone. Mark records Jesus saying, "Go into all the world and preach the gospel to all creation" (Mark 16:15). Among other things, this means that as his disciples, we are to be obedient and do our part in spreading the Good News about Jesus Christ. We are to be people of persuasion, boldly declaring Jesus Christ to be the only way to salvation. The fact that God has chosen to work through us for the fulfillment of his mission in the world is, of course, a great mystery. Since God is sovereign, he is sufficient to accomplish evangelism without human agency. The Godhead is the ultimate agent for mission. The Father planned redemption, the Son carried it out, and the Holy Spirit applies it to the human heart (Eph. 1:3–14). No work of human agents in evangelism and church growth was ever effective without the silent, behind-the-scenes, in-the-heart work of God's Spirit. However, within his sovereignty, God calls us to responsibility for preaching the Good News.

While it is the gospel, the Word of God that saves through the regenerating work of the Holy Spirit (Titus 3:5), how can nonbelievers hear without a preacher (Rom. 10:11–14)? The fact is new believers are no more brought to faith in Jesus Christ apart from human agency than they are redeemed apart from divine grace. Paul explained this to the Thessalonians when he said, "God has chosen you from the beginning for salvation through sanctification by the Spirit and faith in the truth. It was for this He called you through our gospel, that you may gain the glory of our Lord Jesus Christ" (2 Thess. 2:13–14). Note that Paul explains logically that, first, God chooses people for salvation exclusively by divine grace, that is, "through sanctification by the Spirit." Second, he calls people to glory by divinely controlled human agency, that is, "through our gospel."

This passage indicates a threefold process in evangelism. First, the divine choice was in eternity (from the beginning). Second, the divine process of efficacious grace is in time (in the Spirit and belief in the truth). The Spirit's work is tied to the work of the Word. "The Spirit does the work of pre-salvation sanctification. The Word quickens the heart of the believer as it is preached."5 Third, the divine call is "through our gospel." This is where we (human agency) come into the picture. It is *our* gospel; that is, it is ours personally and we share it personally. The gospel is powerful when it is declared in *truth* and *relationship*. In a previous letter to the Thessalonians, Paul reminds them, "our gospel did not come to you in word only, but also in power and in the Holy Spirit and with full conviction; just as you know what kind of men we proved to be among you for your sake" (1 Thess. 1:5). The truth of the gospel (declaration of the facts of the gospel) was preached (personal communication by the speaker) in a dynamic relationship. "From eternity God has chosen a company for Himself and today He is calling them out as a people for His name, but the voice He wants to use is yours and mine."[6] The salvation process is God's operation from beginning to end, but it includes our personal responsibility to share the gospel with those who have yet to believe.

The symbolism of *stewards* and *servants* in the New Testament is rich in this regard. We are called God's fellow workers (1 Cor. 3:9), laboring together with him. The term *fellow worker* is a concept found throughout the New Testament. In all cases, the worker or steward is required to be obedient. For example, in the parable of the talents, the master gives gifts to servants who are considered responsible agents. At the end of each story, the master holds the servants responsible for their obedience or disobedience (Matt. 25:14–30; Luke 19:11–27). Those servants who were obedient received a reward, while the disobedient servants received punishment. Likewise the apostle Paul reminded the Corinthians, "I planted, Apollos watered, but God was causing the growth" (1 Cor. 3:6). God sovereignly brings about the growth of the church through evangelism, but his servants are held responsible to proclaim the Good News of salvation in Christ alone. Paul noted the servant's responsibility when he said, "Now he who plants and he who waters are one; but each will receive his own reward according to his own labor. For we are God's fellow workers" (vv. 8–9). Only God in his sovereignty brings people to faith in Christ, but our role as responsible agents (stewards and servants) is to take specific action to fulfill this calling by preaching the gospel for a verdict.

Preaching for a Verdict

The truth that we now live and function in an extremely diverse religious culture causes some Christians to back away from overt evangelism. Attempting to persuade others that Jesus Christ is the only way to heaven (John 14:6) seems arrogant and old-fashioned. Instead, it is suggested that the best approach is to dialogue with others in an attempt to find the common truth in all faiths, while allowing individuals to come to their own conclusions about truth. Regrettably, the concept of dialogue is quite vague. In the best meaning of the term, *dialogue* suggests a friendly, respectful discussion that seeks to persuade the other person to one's view with a spirit of mutual understanding. In the weakest use of the term, *dialogue* suggests a conversation between people where neither seeks to persuade the other; rather they dialogue purely to communicate. Dialogue becomes nothing but a respectful discussion with no agenda of converting the other person to one's way of thinking or point of view. The first form of dialogue is certainly biblical; that is, we should seek to persuade others with a spirit of understanding. The second concept of dialogue is decidedly not biblical, for Christian witness must always witness for a verdict. In other words, the Christian always seeks to persuade another to believe in Jesus Christ for salvation, accept baptism, and become a responsible part of the church.

Both the Old and New Testaments place belief in God above belief in the gods of this world. The entire Bible presents God as the Creator and Sustainer of the world (Gen. 1:1–2:25; John 1:1–3; Col. 1:16–17). He and he alone is worthy of worship, as God commanded, "You shall have no other gods before Me" (Exod. 20:3). Tragically, humankind is always prone to create other gods to worship, which is why almost the entire Old Testament calls on the nation of Israel to choose between the one true God and the gods of the nations that surround them. Moses prepared Israel to go into the Promised Land and face the many gods that were there, warning them, "Know therefore today, and take it to your heart, that the LORD, He is God in heaven above and on the earth below; there is no other" (Deut. 4:39). It is against this background that the classic battle between Elijah and the prophets of Baal must be viewed (1 Kings 18:20–40). Other gods and religions coexist on earth, but there is just one true God, and everyone must make a choice similar to Joshua's challenge to the people of Israel. "Choose for yourselves today whom you will serve: whether the gods which your fathers served which were beyond the River, or the gods of the Amorites in whose land you are living; but as for me and my house, we will serve the LORD" (Josh. 24:15).

A similar choice is put forth in the New Testament as people are called to make a choice for or against Jesus Christ. "He who believes in Him is not judged; he who does not believe has been judged already, because he has not believed in the name of the only begotten Son of God" (John 3:18). When Jesus declares, "I am the way, and the truth, and the life; no one comes to the Father but through Me" (14:6), he is demanding a verdict. Jesus stressed the need to choose when he asked his disciples, "Who do people say that the Son of Man is?" They answered with a list of possible choices. Then Jesus asked, "But who do you say that I am?" Then Peter gave his powerful confession, "You are the Christ, the Son of the living God" (Matt. 16:13–16). Peter and the disciples had made their choice. Mark ends his Gospel with Jesus's commission, which includes this: "He who has believed and has been baptized shall be saved; but he who has disbelieved shall be condemned" (Mark 16:16). A decision must always be made. Is Jesus Christ the Savior of the world or not?

Early Christian Practice

As stewards of the gospel, the first Christians took action to proclaim salvation in Jesus Christ. Often they approached people in a loving and gracious manner, respectful of their views and options, but always with a desire to call people to make a decision about Christ. Sometimes they just proclaimed the truth, usually with little or no dialogue expected or allowed. Abundant illustration from the early church's experience and practice demonstrates that the gospel was preached with the expectation that a decision or verdict about Jesus Christ would be made. One powerful example occurred on the day of Pentecost. Peter preached in the power of the Holy Spirit and exhorted the people: "Be saved from this perverse generation!" After hearing this, three thousand people decided to follow Christ (Acts 2:40–41). Soon Peter and John suffered arrest for preaching the resurrection of Jesus from the dead when five thousand men "believed" (4:1–4). Others, of course, chose not to follow Jesus, such as the crowd that stoned Stephen (Acts 7). The apostle Paul traveled to Thessalonica, where he proclaimed the resurrection of Christ (17:1–9). "Some of them were persuaded" (v. 4), but others rejected Christ and instead "formed a mob and set the city in an uproar" (v. 5). In Corinth, Paul tried "to persuade Jews and Greeks" by testifying that "Jesus was the Christ" (18:4–5). When Paul was under house arrest in Rome waiting for his day in court, large numbers visited him, and he tried "to persuade them concerning Jesus." He taught people from morning to evening, and "some were being persuaded by the things spoken, but others would not believe" (28:23–24).

Our role in mission is to take responsible action at three levels of evangelism. First, is the level of *presence*. It is at this level that our witness is seen in good deeds and actions of love for others. Presence evangelism lays the foundation for the remaining levels of evangelism, which is why Jesus emphasized letting our light shine before mankind so that they might *see* our good works and glorify our Father in heaven (see Matt. 5:16). Immediately before Jesus tells us to let our light shine, he illustrates his thinking with salt and light (vv. 13–15). Our good deeds make us both salt and light to the world, thus preparing the way for further evangelism. The witness of works is basic to the witness of words.

> *As stewards of the gospel, our role is to take action to proclaim salvation in Jesus Christ.*

Helping people in the name of Christ is Golden Rule–type living, that is, "treat[ing] people the same way you want them to treat you" (Matt. 7:12). Loving your neighbor as yourself is always in season and appropriate (Luke 10:25–27).

This missional approach to evangelism is biblical, but some believe nothing more is required. They see the goal of presence evangelism as simply loving and helping others. Hence, evangelism becomes anything good the church does outside its four walls. *Evangelism*, however, is not an umbrella term for everything good the church does in the world. We must, of course, feed the hungry, teach immigrants to read English, help the oppressed, promote civil rights, treat the environment with care, visit the sick, care for the aged, and denounce social injustice. But all these good works are not the end of evangelism, they are just the foundation for it. Being present among non-believers is just part of the normal Christian life and witness, but it's just the beginning of the mission of proclaiming the Good News of salvation in Christ and gaining a verdict for him. We must move on to the next level of evangelism.

> *The witness of works is basic to the witness of words.*

The second level is *proclamation*. At this level, good words are added to good deeds. The apostle Paul asks four questions in Romans 10:14–15. First, how are people to call upon him in whom they have not believed? Second, how are they to believe in him of whom they have not heard? Third, how are they to hear without a preacher? And, fourth, how are people to preach unless they are sent? The point of all four questions is that the gospel must be proclaimed not just practiced!

The goal of proclamation evangelism is to help people understand and respond to the gospel of forgiveness and life in Jesus Christ. It calls people to make a verdict for or against Jesus Christ. Some stop at this level. They feel that if the gospel is clearly proclaimed, and people have been given a chance to decide, their job is finished. But our role does not end with proclaiming the gospel.

The third level of evangelism is *persuasion*. Our role at this level is to persuade people to go beyond a decision to believe on Jesus for their salvation. This results in disciples for Christ, rather than just converts. It fulfills the goal of the Great Commission to "make disciples." How does this happen? Matthew 28:19–20 lists three verbs (participles) that tell us how to make disciples: going, baptizing, and teaching. Thus our role is to *go* with the gospel, *baptize* those who repent and believe, and *teach* those who continue to follow Christ. A disciple is a learner who voluntarily submits to the teaching of another person. Being a disciple of Jesus Christ means we place ourselves under his teaching and become like him.

The gospel must be proclaimed not just practiced.

What is our role? In general it is to be actively proclaiming the gospel of salvation in Jesus Christ. Specifically, our role varies with each level of evangelism. At the *presence* level, our role is to connect with nonbelievers by witnessing in deed. Among other things, this includes engaging in ministries of social action, meeting felt needs, and providing loving care as appropriate in our communities. At the *proclamation* level, our role is to preach the gospel by witnessing in word. Among other things, this involves sharing our faith journey, telling others about Jesus Christ, and teaching the Bible in various ways. At the *persuasion* level, our role is to persuade others by witnessing in reasoned argument. Among other things, this involves listening to others and offering reasonable response and logical debate. In reality, some of us are more skilled at presence evangelism and enjoy building caring relationships with nonbelievers. Some find they are more fruitful at proclamation evangelism and feel comfortable elucidating the Good News of salvation in Jesus Christ. Others are more successful at persuasion evangelism and are energized by convincing people to believe.

We are "servants of Christ and stewards of the mysteries of God" (1 Cor. 4:1) and are expected to be obedient and proclaim the gospel in a manner that calls for a verdict. Whatever means we use to proclaim, whether it is *presence*, *proclamation*, or *persuasion*, the expectation is that, when we invite people to become Christ's followers, our hearers must make a decision for or against Christ. We are called to a role of active proclamation of the gospel—a proclamation with an invitation to accept or reject Jesus Christ. With this understanding, there is no such thing as a silent witness. We must use words. Modeling a good Christian lifestyle is just the foundation. No one ever came to Christ without some sort of proclamation and persuasion. We are called to present the Good News for acceptance. God calls people through people, for "we are ambassadors for Christ, as though God were making an appeal through us; we beg you on behalf of Christ, be reconciled to God" (2 Cor. 5:20). This is our role. May we be obedient.

Levels of Evangelism

Presence Evangelism
- Goal: Helping others in the name of the Lord.
- Evaluation: How many people have been helped?

Proclamation Evangelism
- Goal: Helping others hear about and decide to believe in Jesus Christ as their personal Savior.
- Evaluation: How many people have believed?

Persuasion Evangelism
- Goal: Helping others become disciples of Jesus Christ.
- Evaluation: How many people have become lifelong followers of Jesus Christ?

Probing Questions

1. Which levels of evangelism are strongest in your church?
2. Which level or levels are missing or need some work?
3. How many people did you help last year? How many people believed in Christ through your church last year? How many new disciples were made in your church last year?

5

What Is Our Focus?

The night had been a rough one. None of the disciples had gotten much sleep. Everything for which they had hoped and about which they had dreamed and fantasized did not occur. Some were completely distraught, while others sat quietly immersed in their own thoughts. No one spoke; no one knew what to say. Jesus had died, and most of his followers had scattered from the scene in fear or confusion. A few of the women, and perhaps John and Nicodemus, stayed until Jesus was taken down from the cross and placed in Joseph of Arimathea's tomb. No one knew what the morning would bring. Would the soldiers come for them, or would their small band of disciples be ignored, eventually to drift away aimlessly into the distant memories of the politicians, religious leaders, and people?

The early morning news brought even more uncertainty. Something dramatic had taken place. When Mary Magdalene and the other Mary went out to see the tomb, an earthquake made the ground shake, and the women encountered an angel who told them that Jesus was alive. Quickly they returned to tell the gathered disciples. On hearing the news, Peter and John went to see the tomb and found it empty. The gossip around town whispered that the disciples had come and stolen the body of Jesus, but the disciples knew that story was untrue. Could it be that Jesus was actually alive, or was it simply that the soldiers had taken his body and hidden it? The women told the disciples that Jesus wanted them to go to Galilee to see him, but before they could leave, Jesus appeared to them too.

Like many well-loved accounts, the Gospel of Matthew is epic. It describes the life of a hero who appeared on the scene to fulfill the expectations and hopes of his people. Evil people within the country, who sought to destroy his good efforts to establish a just and loving kingdom, challenged him. The challenge resulted in what appeared at first to be a victory for the evil opposition, but then without warning, the hero arose in a great triumph to win the day.

The role of Jesus as the hero, indeed Savior, of the world is presented quickly in the Gospel of Matthew. His name is Jesus, which means "He will save His people from their sins" (Matt. 1:21). This is an assertion that Jesus's role in the divine plan of salvation is one of good news. He gave his life "a ransom for many" (20:28), and his story is to be diffused throughout the world. For this to happen, he must have followers, so he called a group of fishermen and others, who left their various jobs and professions to become an itinerant band of disciples. His disciples were differentiated from the multitudes of people who gathered around him (4:25). Often he went away from the crowds to spend time alone with his disciples to teach them. Over time he narrowed the disciples to just a few, primarily twelve, whom he called apostles (10:2). As soon as Jesus chose the apostles, he informed them that the harvest was ready (9:37–38).

Jesus's disciples were inspired by his compassion for the multitudes (v. 36). He directed them to speak to the lost sheep of the house of Israel (10:6) because at that time the Twelve had so little training and were not ready to go to the Samaritans and the Gentiles. Eventually they were commissioned to go to the ends of the world, following his death and resurrection (28:18–20). The mission was multiethnic and cross-cultural. The fact that the disciples initially focused narrowly on the house of Israel simply points out that they were not ready for the emergence of the formal commission of Christ at this point in their development. Gradually Jesus expanded their experiences and slowly enlarged their vision. By the time he made his final address on the mountain in Galilee, the disciples had expanded insight and experience. They were now ready for cross-cultural mission, which Christ gave them in the form of a command. They were truly ready to be fishers of men (4:19).

At the prearranged time, the disciples made their way to Galilee to the mountain where they had spent other times with Jesus. When he appeared, some worshiped him and others doubted it was really him, but they all wondered what Jesus was going to say. The final words someone speaks are often held in high regard, and this situation felt promising. Perhaps Jesus was now going to establish his earthly kingdom. They had hoped for such an occurrence for many years. Was Jesus going to tell them to feed the hungry? There were many hungry people, and Jesus had once fed more than five thousand people with just a few fish and a few pieces of bread. Might he say clothe the naked? Many poor people had little to wear, and clothing them would be most welcome. Would he say heal the sick? Everyone saw sick people sitting on the sides of the roads, in the town centers, and at the healing pools of water, such as at Bethesda. What about the people who were held unjustly in the prisons? Might Jesus tell them to fight for their release? Each anticipated his words, but he addressed none of these issues. Instead, he announced, "All authority has been given to Me in heaven and on earth. Go therefore and make disciples of all the nations, baptizing them in the name of the Father and the Son and the Holy Spirit, teaching them to observe all that I commanded you; and lo, I am with you always, even to the end of the age" (28:19–20).

Great Truths

Some form of Jesus's commission is found at the end of all four Gospels and in the beginning of Acts and is mentioned by Paul in Romans 16:25–26. Matthew's account is most well-known, however, and is called the Great Commission. This is proper, for the whole story of Jesus moves with tremendous power to the closing words of the Gospel of Matthew. The final words of Jesus are striking along several lines of thought. First is the idea of *authority*. Jesus Christ was given all power because of his victory over sin and death. The fact that he had resurrection power meant that the commission to make disciples was no mere hope or dream or fantasy, that is, a commission that cannot be fulfilled. The disciples were not listening to an itinerate preacher or a lowly carpenter. They were now hearing the words of the resurrected Christ who defeated death and was about to ascend to the throne room of God to sit at the Father's right hand (Acts 1:9–11; Rom. 8:34; Eph. 1:20; Heb. 1:3; 8:1). His final words carried a ring of power that the Twelve may have missed previously but now Jesus made very clear. His authority was unlimited, a fact noted in the phrase "in heaven and on earth" (Matt. 28:18). Jesus has authority over all things in heaven, all things on earth, and everything in between.

The second feature of the Great Commission is that it has a *clear focus*—make disciples! A disciple is a student who acquires knowledge from a teacher. It is an exceptional word, used only a few times in the New Testament, and implies not only gaining knowledge but also living out what is learned. The command is explicit and means the followers of Jesus (disciples) are to enroll others in his school so they can be learners (disciples) too.

Prophetic anticipation is the third feature seen in Christ's Great Commission. The disciples were sent with the authority of the Lord on apostolic mission. They were to make disciples of "all the nations." *Nations* is best understood to refer to the tribes, families, and peoples of the world. It reverberates with the promise of God to Abram: "In you all the families of the earth will be blessed" (Gen. 12:3). It is an ongoing commission that will in time result in every people group, family, and clan on the earth having the opportunity to be disciples of Jesus Christ.

The fourth feature is the *rhythm* of the Great Commission. Jesus's command to make disciples, while clear, left the twelve disciples with the question of how to go about obeying. Fortunately Jesus explained the question of *means* in the three words (participles in original Greek) that surround the central command. There is progression—rhythm—in this, for the first thing to do is to go. "Go" is correctly read as an imperative, since it takes on the action of the command to make disciples. The twelve disciples, and others, had no choice but to go if they were to fulfill the command to make disciples of all the nations. It rightly refers to evangelistic proclamation and, as such, is the first movement in the rhythm of the Great Commission. Without going, there is never obedient teaching. Without going, there is never any baptism. Without going, there is no disciple making. Going is communicating the good news that Jesus lived a sinless life, died on the cross, and rose the third day in victory over death. He is God and the only Savior of the world—the only way to eternal life.

The second rhythmic step is *baptizing*, as those who believe in Jesus Christ publically identify with, primarily, his death, burial, and resurrection and, secondarily, with the rest of his disciples. The rhythm of baptism bonds new disciples to the person of Christ and his fellowship on earth—the church. It asks new believers to submit to Christ's leadership and ties them to a community of faith where they may be taught, held accountable, and grow.

Then follows the third phase in the rhythm of the Great Commission. Once a person has received Christ and has been baptized, they are *taught to obey* all things (everything) that Christ instructed. Evangelism (the going) and assimilation (the baptizing) is to culminate in maturing disciples. This spiritual formation goes beyond knowledge to obedient living. It is a process that keeps the work of disciple making going, for "everything" surely includes going and baptizing, which completes the rhythm of the Great Commission.

The fifth feature of the Great Commission is that it *continues to the end of the age*. Jesus promised his divine presence with his disciples in mission to the end of the age. This is often ignored, but Jesus made it quite specific. The Great Commission is ongoing, from the first coming of Christ until he returns. Theologically we reside in the same period as the early disciples, that is, between the resurrection of Jesus and his return. Since there is no record of the Great Commission ever being rescinded, terminated, or withdrawn, we must conclude that Jesus expects us to obey it today!

Maturing Disciples

The goal of the Great Commission is to make disciples. Unfortunately some take this to mean making better disciples or healthier Christians of those who are already in the church, that is, making older believers maturer. A look at current and past literature regarding disciple making demonstrates that such literature rarely includes evangelism and assimilation of people into a local church. All churches and pastors see their ministry as a teaching ministry, and this leads churches to place an emphasis on maturing those who already attend worship. This is regularly expressed as a need for the spiritual formation of God's people, a focus that rarely, if ever, includes the proclamation of the saving gospel of salvation. The underlying supposition of spiritual formation implies that if Christians will become more spiritual, they will naturally reach out to share their faith with others. To some proponents of spiritual formation, evangelism is just a superficial activity, and any effort to add to a church's membership is suspect, even considered a wrong form of proselytizing. The more important activity, some say, is to strengthen the meditative life of the saints. Thus many pastors work, pray, and agonize over their current church worshipers; they want to improve their biblical literacy, increase their time in prayer, and generally make them better Christians. Pastors try to revive or revitalize the spiritual lives of complacent disciples, to help them become full of the Holy Spirit and live in the fullness of their Christian faith. While this sometimes results in new disciples being made, in most cases, it does not. In more than a few cases, it results in local churches ignoring their responsibility to evangelize and assimilate new disciples into the life of the church.

Conversely we have the Great Commission's call to make disciples, which is only fulfilled when *new* disciples are made out of secular humanity. The Great Commission demands numerical growth of Christ's church through the winning of new converts and folding them into local churches. It is true that we need spiritual formation of all disciples, but we must focus on making many new disciples as well. The focus cannot be either/or. It must be both/and. "To seek quantity without attending to quality is to neglect the teaching clause of the Great Commission. To seek quality without quantity neglects the scope of the Great Commission."[1]

The Great Commission demands numerical growth of Christ's church.

Certainly there is a great need in the church today for a revival of spiritual life, but not an introverted spirituality that ignores evangelism. Today is not the time for such an inverted spiritual formation. If spiritual formation is to be a continuing, effective force, it must bring fresh thinking and resources to bear on empowering effective evangelism. Spiritual formation that does not result in intense efforts to win people to faith in Christ and into responsible membership in his church is truncated. The call to spiritual formation must include a focus on all three rhythms of evangelizing new disciples, adding new disciples to a local church, and nurturing new disciples toward maturity. Spiritual formation of those who are currently obeying is actually helped by streams of newly converted disciples entering our churches. As missiologist Donald McGavran noted, "Multitudes of new Christians feeding on the word, nurtured by the Fellowship of the church, and available to the Holy Spirit are the surest way to renewal." Our focus must be on making disciples, which includes a balanced emphasis on evangelism, assimilation, and spiritual formation.

The Great Commission cannot be carried on without the corporate fellowship found in the church. Following the giving of the Great Commission, Christ left a band of believers—the church—with a commission to preach the gospel, connect new believers to the group, and grow in spiritual maturity. There is a relationship between making disciples and the corporate group. The *group* is to go, the *group* is to baptize, and the *group* is to teach. Maturity into full discipleship takes place in Christ's body, the local church.

Probing Questions

1. To what degree should evangelism and spiritual formation be balanced in a local church?
2. How would you describe the importance of assimilation as the bridge between evangelism and spiritual formation?
3. Should any of the three rhythms of the Great Commission receive greater emphasis than the others? Why or why not?

6

What Is Our Context?

It had been nearly seven days since Jesus ascended into the heavens. The followers of Jesus numbered around 120 people. No doubt there were other people in town somewhere who still believed in Jesus, perhaps just too afraid to associate with his small band of followers. Each day dragged by as the disciples hoped against hope. When was Jesus going to send his helper? When was his promised power going to come?

Someone suggested they needed to find a replacement for Judas, who had betrayed Jesus. Peter, who normally was the spokesperson for the twelve disciples, said the person chosen to replace Judas must be someone who had been with them from the time of John the Baptist until Jesus's ascension. The names of Barsabbas and Matthias were put forward. After prayer and discussion, the disciples chose Matthias, completing the group once again.

On the day of Pentecost, they suddenly heard a rushing wind, and it filled the house where they were living. The disciples were filled with the Holy Spirit and started speaking in other languages, because the Holy Spirit was empowering them to do so. The thousands of people gathered in Jerusalem for the Pentecost celebration heard what had happened to the disciples and gathered around, surprised that they could hear what was spoken in their own individual languages and dialects. Peter stood up in a place where he could be heard and spoke to all the people who were gathered. He talked with confidence as he confronted the people about their responsibility for the death of Jesus. The people who listened intently were convicted regarding Jesus and asked what they should do. Peter admonished them that they needed to believe and be baptized in the name of Jesus Christ because of their remission of sins. The response was large, as three thousand people believed, were baptized, and were added to the church in Jerusalem.

The Great Commission is a corporate commission and can be fulfilled only as God's people, his church, work together to carry it out.

Today some church leaders say it is not about the church but about the kingdom. Jesus, of course, spoke often of the kingdom, but he told his twelve disciples that he would build his church (Matt. 16:18). The Great Commission is a corporate commission and can be fulfilled only as God's people, his church, work together to carry it out.

Jesus never conceived an autonomous commission. From the very beginning, he gathered around him a crowd of people, out of which he selected individual followers, whom he eventually called disciples. Throughout his earthly ministry, Jesus revealed the interrelationship of mission and the idea of a corporate group of people. Jesus and his band of followers had many discussions and shared experiences of mission (12:1; 13:10, 36; 14:15). Gradually as the work matured, they began to see Jesus as the Christ, the Messiah for whom they were looking, and he prepared them for the shock of his death on the cross. They were part of significant experiences, such as the transfiguration, the triumphal entry, the last week of Jesus's life, the time in Gethsemane, and their fear and confusion following the cross. All of these experiences and events served to bond them into a cohesive group that hung together in the difficult hours, ultimately participating in Jesus's final commissioning to carry the gospel to the world.

Jesus's Promise

As they waited in the upper room, the 120 believers began to organize themselves. Leadership emerged initially in the person of Peter, and finally they received the power of the Holy Spirit for witnessing. With the salvation and incorporation of 3,000 new believers into the church, the small band of 120 disciples grew exponentially to a size that could do what the Great Commission demanded—make disciples of Jesus Christ. Thinking back, the disciples no doubt recalled Jesus's words recorded in Matthew 16:18. Jesus had just asked the disciples who they thought he was when Peter answered, "You are the Christ, the Son of the living God" (Matt. 16:16). After this Jesus said to them, "I will build My church" (v. 18). Jesus's use of the word *church* here was the first time the word was used in the New Testament. Now, as the disciples looked back on the day of Pentecost, they had a clearer understanding of what Christ was implying.

Jesus was anticipating the establishment of Christian churches after the coming of the Holy Spirit on the day of Pentecost. In its historical usage, *church* (Greek: *ekklesia*) simply meant "an assembly," that is, a physical gathering of people. Over several years, the word took on the technical meaning of a Christian assembly, with the implication of physical unity and spiritual unity. At the same time, the word took on a larger metaphorical meaning, often described as the *spiritual*, *universal*, or *invisible* church. For example, Luke wrote, "A great persecution began against the church in Jerusalem" (Acts 8:1), with the result that Christians were scattered throughout Judea and Samaria. Later, after Saul (now Paul) became a believer in Christ, Luke reported, "So the church throughout all Judea and Galilee and Samaria enjoyed peace, being built up; and going on in the fear of the Lord and in the comfort of the Holy Spirit, it continued to increase" (9:31). Obviously Luke was speaking of a large metaphorical concept of church, for one physical church cannot be in three places at once. The term *church* in Matthew 16:18 likely refers to the entirety of the new entity. It embodies *both* the larger body of Christ, as well as local assemblies of believers.

The church has three characteristics. First, it belongs to Jesus. Emphatically, Jesus said "my" church. Christ's church is different from any previous assembly of people. It is not a synagogue; rather, it is an assemblage of people who have a unique relationship to him. Second, the church is going to be something new. When Jesus said I "will build" he meant that he would build it in the future. It was something that was still in the future, not to be confused with his earthly band of disciples. Third, the church was going to be permanent. "The gates of Hades will not overpower it" is generally accepted to mean the church will not die. Since local assemblies do die, Jesus must have been referencing the larger universal nature of the church. It is not just that the church will not die, but as gates are a defensive structure, the inference is that the church is on the move. It is an advancing church, ever growing as people accept Jesus Christ as their Savior and become active participants in a local assembly.

That understood, the seeds of the local church must also be seen in the passage, a fact that seems clear from the only other usage of the word in the Gospels in Matthew 18:17. In this passage addressing church discipline, Jesus encouraged believers who have observed a person sin to first talk to the individual face-to-face, and if he does not listen, to then speak to him with one or two other people. If the person still does not listen, Jesus said, "tell it to the church; and if he refuses to listen even to the church, let him be to you as a Gentile and a tax collector." In this passage Jesus was not talking about his small band of disciples, for they did not have the constituted authority to execute discipline. The church Jesus was speaking about must be an organized assembly of believers with the spiritual and constitutional authority to execute discipline. This seems most clear in verse 20 of the same passage. "For where two or three have gathered together in My name, I am there in their midst" implies the future when Jesus is physically away from his disciples yet spiritually present with his church anywhere it is assembled. While Jesus did form a band of disciples, they had no formal organization. It was a prophetic band, pointing to the future when Jesus was going to establish his church following the coming of the Holy Spirit on the day of Pentecost.

Kingdom or Church

When people open the New Testament and read through the Gospels, they will find the word *kingdom* (Greek: *basileia*) constantly used, while the word *church* occurs only three times. In the first three Gospels, Matthew used the word *kingdom* fifty-four times, Mark nineteen times, and Luke forty-four times. John mentioned *kingdom* just three times. Jesus spoke much about the kingdom of God and the kingdom of heaven. The kingdom of God most often refers to Jesus's reign after his return to earth at his second coming. The kingdom of heaven is a phrase found only Matthew's Gospel (thirty-one times) and once in Revelation. Matthew used *kingdom of heaven*, most likely in deference to Jewish sensibilities. The kingdom of heaven looks primarily at the interval between Jesus's rejection by the Jewish nation as their Messiah and his return to earth in glory. Thus in Matthew Jesus is announcing to the Jewish populace that the long anticipated kingdom will be postponed until Israel acknowledges Christ's lordship (see Zech. 12:10 and Matt. 23:39).[1] On the day of Jesus's ascension, the gathered disciples asked, "Lord, is it at this time You are restoring the kingdom to Israel? (Acts 1:6).

The question of the relationship between the kingdom and the church has endured almost since the first disciples watched Jesus Christ ascend into heaven. Throughout church history, at least since the time of Augustine, it has been common for people to identify kingdom and church as the same.

This view led naturally to the establishment of the Roman Catholic Church and Protestant state churches. Nevertheless, the gradual development of religious freedom following the Protestant Reformation in both Europe and North America led to the breakdown of this view. Today there is some agreement that the kingdom is both present and yet to come. But confusion continues over the relationship between kingdom and church. In fact, it is common to hear pastors say, "It's about the kingdom, not about the church." Unfortunately this statement, and others similar to it, is not clearly defined. What is meant by *kingdom*? What is meant by *church*? In general, such statements appear to mean that Christians and churches should not be in competition with each other because they are all working toward the same end. To this, most can generally agree. It is of great importance that people come to faith in Jesus Christ (an eternal decision) but less important into which denominational family they assimilate (a temporal decision).[2] The true battle is not one Christian denomination or church group against another, but a culture and resistant people increasingly antagonistic toward the church.

While it is true that we are not fighting each other, there are good reasons to understand that *kingdom* and *church* are different—and that it *is* about the church. First, even though the word *church* is used 114 times in the New Testament, it is never identified with the kingdom. Second, Jesus could have said, "I will build my kingdom," but he did not. He did, of course, say, "I will build my church," which is greatly different. When Jesus said my church, he was making a contrast with the kingdom, which was just announced as "the" kingdom. He is saying that his church must be built, and the gates of Hades will not overpower it; neither of these statements are ever made about the kingdom. Third, the idea of *kingdom* was offered to Israel as being "at hand" (Matt. 3:2; 4:17). Concerning the church Jesus said, "I will build," that is, at that time it was still in the future (16:18). The kingdom was an old theme; the church was a new theme. Fourth, the theme of *kingdom* increasingly gave way to the theme of *church* as the apostles and early disciples carried out the Great Commission. The last recorded question the disciples asked of Jesus before he ascended into heaven was, "Lord, is it at this time You are restoring the kingdom to Israel?" (Acts 1:6). Jesus's answer to his disciples' inquiry did not deny a future establishment of the kingdom, but he told them it was not for them to know when it would happen (v. 7). Then Jesus turned their attention toward his commission by saying, "You will receive power when the Holy Spirit has come upon you; and you shall be My witnesses both in Jerusalem, and in all Judea and Samaria, and even to the remotest part of the earth" (v. 8). With this statement, Jesus directed the attention of his disciples from kingdom to church. Throughout the rest of Acts, the momentum moves increasingly away from kingdom as the center of interest and to the church being central. From that time on through the third chapter of Revelation, *church* is the central theme. It is striking that all of the Epistles, and even the letters in chapters 2 and 3 of Revelation, are directed to churches or members of churches. The theme of *kingdom* is once again taken up in the fourth chapter of Revelation as future apocalyptic events and the coming of the theocratic King are revealed.

It *Is* about the Church

The actions of the apostles and early disciples point to the fact that our mission today *is* about the church. After the outpouring of the Holy Spirit on the day of Pentecost, Peter's preaching focused on Jesus Christ's death, burial, and resurrection (Acts 2:23–24). He called the people to repentance and baptism, "and that day there were added about three thousand souls" (v. 41). We must ask, added to what? The only answer is the church, the church at Jerusalem. The church "that day" was both universal and local, perhaps the only time the two were exactly the same, as the church grew quickly in numbers after that. Just a few days later, Peter and John participated in the healing of a lame man, after which Peter preached the death and resurrection of Jesus (3:15; 4:2) and the need to believe in his name (3:19), and five thousand believed (4:4).

Soon after, the need for church discipline arose when Ananias and Sapphira lied to the Holy Spirit and died as a result (5:1–11). "Great fear came over the whole church" (v. 11), but the church continued to grow as "believers in the Lord, multitudes of men and women, were constantly added to their number" (v. 14).

Organizational issues became obvious as the church grew in complexity. The apostles set goals for the ministry and reorganized the work so "the word of God kept on spreading; and the number of the disciples continued to increase greatly in Jerusalem" (6:7). In all of its growth, the early church demonstrated obvious signs that the believers worked together as a corporate unit. There was a doctrinal standard, fellowship, baptism, public worship, giving to the needy, communion, and organizational structure (Acts 2:42–47; 6:1–7). All are indicators of an organized local church, even if it was loosely organized.

The theme of the kingdom did not go away quickly. Evidence shows that the apostles did not proclaim the reign of

Jesus, but rather the death, burial, and resurrection of Jesus. Following the martyrdom of Stephen, Saul instigated a great persecution of the church in Jerusalem. Many believers scattered and "went about preaching the word" (8:4). Philip was "preaching the good news about the kingdom of God and the name of Jesus Christ" (v. 12), with the result that many men and women believed and were baptized. Later Philip "preached Jesus" (v. 35) to the Ethiopian eunuch, who also believed and was baptized. The context implies that Philip preached the same message that Peter and John had earlier preached in Jerusalem, that is, the death, burial, and resurrection of Jesus Christ. The message of the kingdom was changing into the message of salvation through Christ alone.

When Paul taught in the synagogue at Ephesus, Luke wrote that he was "reasoning and persuading them about the kingdom of God" (19:8). The exact content of his preaching is not known, but apparently he was preaching the message of salvation in Jesus. Some responded by "speaking evil of the Way" (v. 9), while "the name of the Lord Jesus was being magnified" by others (v. 17). In all cases "the word of the Lord was growing mightily and prevailing" (v. 20), which is a metaphor for the growth of the churches. Again, the context appears to imply that Paul's message of the kingdom of God was more about the death, burial, and resurrection of Jesus than his kingdom reign. At the end of Paul's life, he was held for two full years, and people were allowed to come and talk with him. During this time, he was "preaching the kingdom of God and teaching concerning the Lord Jesus Christ" (28:31). Given Paul's knowledge of the Old Testament, he likely had discussions about what the kingdom of God entailed, but the addition of the phrases "trying to persuade them concerning Jesus" (v. 23) and "teaching concerning the Lord Jesus Christ" (v. 31) to the words "preaching the kingdom of God" suggests the content included the message of salvation. This probability is increased, given the fact that in 1 Corinthians 15:1–2 Paul points precisely to the message he preached. He called the Corinthians to remember the gospel he preached to them.

> For I delivered to you as of first importance what I also received, that Christ died for our sins according to the Scriptures, and that He was buried, and that He was raised on the third day according to the Scriptures, and that He appeared to Cephas, then to the twelve. After that He appeared to more than five hundred brethren at one time, most of whom remain until now, but some have fallen asleep; then He appeared to James, then to all the apostles; and last of all, as to one untimely born, He appeared to me also.
>
> 1 Corinthians 15:3–8

The message of the four Gospels that the kingdom of God is near was gradually replaced with the message of salvation through Christ alone. Indeed, the gospel of salvation is the way into the kingdom of God. Speaking to the Colossians, Paul stated that he and Timothy gave thanks for them because of their faith "in Christ Jesus," obtained through "the word of truth, the gospel" (Col. 1:3–5). Paul mentioned that the same word of truth is "constantly bearing fruit and increasing" in all the world (v. 6), which means that people were believing in Jesus Christ and churches were being started. Through faith in Jesus Christ, the Father has "rescued us from the domain of darkness, and transferred us to the kingdom of His beloved Son, in whom we have redemption, the forgiveness of sins" (vv. 13–14).

It is in the church that the glory of God is made manifest. In Paul's letter to the Ephesians, the topic of the church is found extensively. The word *church* is found nine times, and the word *body*, a metaphor for the church, also occurs nine times. The church as a diverse body of individuals, both Jew and Gentile, was a newly revealed mystery. The mystery was unknown to past generations, namely that "Gentiles are fellow heirs and fellow members of the body and fellow partakers of the promise in Christ Jesus through the gospel" (Eph. 3:6). Referring to his own salvation, Paul noted that he was given grace "to preach to the Gentiles the unfathomable riches of Christ" (v. 8), specifically this mystery of the church, "so that the manifold wisdom of God might now be made known through the church to the rulers and the authorities in the heavenly places" (v. 10). The multifaceted wisdom of God is made known through the church! It is about the church. Our context for mission is in the church and not the kingdom per se. Certainly the kingdom is a larger concept than that of church, but for us today, we are doing mission with a focus on church rather than kingdom.

The glory of God is made manifest in the church.

The church is Christ's body, and through it, he displays his wisdom. As the church proclaims the saving gospel of Jesus Christ, it prepares people for the kingdom by bringing them into a right relationship with the coming King. Thus the present task of the church is to make disciples, which includes gospel proclamation and assimilation of new believers into local churches where they may begin the process of spiritual formation. So how is the church doing? How are people actually coming to Christ and his church? The answers to this and other questions are found in chapter 7.

Probing Questions

1. Why did the word *church* gradually replace the word *kingdom* in the New Testament Epistles?
2. What does the phrase "It's about the kingdom not the church" communicate to you? Why?
3. How is doing mission in the context of church different than in the context of kingdom?

Part 2

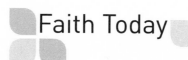

Faith Today

7

Who Led You to Faith in Christ?

"Bob McMahan is the best small-group leader I've ever had," Teresa shared as she sipped a cup of tea. "Actually, I guess I'm biased because he's also the person who prayed with me when I received Christ."

"That's wonderful. I think we always have a fondness for the person who led us to faith," Gloria said with a smile. "In my case, it was my mother. I was only a child, but I still remember her kneeling with me beside my bed as we prayed together."

"My experience is a little different from both of yours," Marge interjected. "As you know, I wasn't much of a church-goer before I came to Journey Church. In fact, I hadn't been to church in more than twenty years."

"Really?" Teresa asked. "I had no idea."

"Really!" Marge confirmed with a look of resolve. "But fortunately I met Mary Rutherford at my Tuesday/Thursday exercise class. We started having lunch on Tuesdays, and she invited me to Journey's Friday morning women's Bible study. That's where I learned that I needed to put my trust in Jesus Christ for salvation. I'd say it was my friend Mary who is most responsible for my believing in Jesus.

"It took several conversations with our associate pastor before my husband placed his faith in Christ," Marge added. "It's interesting that someone different was involved in each of our lives at a vital moment."

"Yes, it is," Teresa and Gloria replied in unison. "Let's ask some of our other friends who was responsible for bringing them to Christ and talk about what we find out when we meet next week," Teresa suggested before she took one last sip of tea. "It might be interesting."

Yes, it is an interesting question, and one that has just recently been studied seriously. Since the days of the First Great Awakening (1730–1740) in what was called the New World and the Second Great Awakening (1790–1820) following the American Revolution, it has generally been assumed by church leaders that people come to faith through church revivals, mass crusades, and chance encounters. The Great Awakenings in the New World and England produced well-known evangelists like John and Charles Wesley, Jonathan Edwards, George Whitefield, Francis Asbury, and Charles Finney, to name a few. Often these men drew crowds numbering in the thousands, and many new believers were added to the church during their time. Over the ensuing years, other high-profile evangelists came to prominence in North America, men such as Dwight L. Moody, Billy Sunday, and most recently Billy Graham. During the early growth years of the United States, Baptist, Methodist, and independent church pastors and laypersons crisscrossed the frontier and rural environments, knocking on doors, winning the common folks to Christ, and planting new churches. These activities led to a developed lore that the way to do evangelism was through mass events, church revivals, camp meetings, home visitations, and cold calling. Of course there was some underlying truth in the body of traditions that developed around evangelistic activity. However, no one actually knew how people were coming to Christ and his church since no one took the time to investigate the facts.

A missionary in India, Donald A. McGavran, first explored this topic and published his findings in 1955 in *The Bridges of God*. McGavran wrote his book in the hope that it might "shed light on the process of how peoples become Christian."[1] He discovered that people in India did not come to faith through revivals, mass crusades, or chance encounters. Rather, they came largely through family relationships and friendships, what he called the "Bridges of God." As he might put it today, we are the bridges over which others walk to find salvation in Jesus Christ. Predictively, North American church leaders did not read his book, as it was primarily for missionaries and mission executives.

It was twenty-five years before church growth pioneer Win Arn, building on the initial discoveries of Donald McGavran, conducted one of the largest studies of how people come to faith in Christ and to the church in the United States and Canada. Arn's Institute for American Church Growth surveyed more than seventeen thousand persons in 1980, asking, "What or who was responsible for your coming to Christ and to your church?"[2] Arn published his findings in *The Master's Plan for Making Disciples*,[3] and church leaders were astounded. He reported that people gave the following eight responses:

Friend/Relative	75–90%
Pastor	5–6%
Sunday School	4–5%
Church Program	2–3%
Walk-In	2–3%
Special Need	1–2%
Visitation	1–2%
Crusade	0.25–0.50%

In one report the institute proclaimed, "The great majority of people today trace their 'spiritual roots' directly to a friend or a relative as the major reason they are now in Christ and their church."[4]

Echoes of Arn's study have reverberated among churches for more than three decades. His findings continue to be quoted in lectures, cited in publications, and presented by church leaders. But in the early 2000s I started noticing that people's testimonies no longer matched Arn's statistics as closely as they once did. Thus at the beginning of the twenty-first century, I engaged in a new study to discover the answer to two key questions—how are people coming to faith in Christ, and how are people coming into responsible church involvement? Eventually my study involved surveys of more than one thousand people in forty-three states.[5] The survey was distributed to people who had been attending a church for two years or less. Some of the respondents had been Christians for several years, while others had made a personal commitment to faith in Christ within two years prior to completing the survey. Those who had made recent commitments are designated in this study as "new converts."

So what did I find? How are people coming to Christ today?

Family and Friends

Family and friends are still the main link for bringing others to faith in Christ, although it is not as high a percentage as it once was. In answer to the question, "What person was it that led you to faith in Christ?" 43.2 percent named a family member and 15.7 percent a friend, for a combined total of 58.9 percent (see graph below).

The Person Who Led Me to Faith in Christ

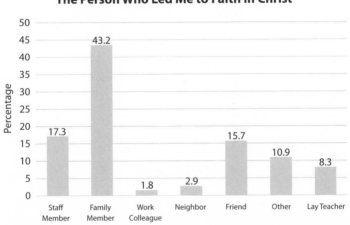

Clearly, family relationships are the primary means by which people come to Christ. The influence of family is two and one-half times more impactful than that of pastoral staff members and three times more than that of friends. Even in a day and time when the idea of family is undergoing significant change, family relationships remain the primary bridge people traverse on their journey to faith in Christ.

The surprising finding is the increased number of people identifying pastoral staff as those who led them to Christ. The Arn study found that pastors accounted for around 6 percent of decisions for Christ, but this recent study shows this number has risen to 17.3 percent. This is nearly a 190 percent increase. Pastors have always led people to personal faith, but their influence in this activity has expanded over the past decades.

Lay teachers account for 8.3 percent of conversions to Christ. This category includes Sunday school teachers, Bible study leaders, small group leaders, VBS teachers, Awana leaders, camp speakers, Good News Bible Club instructors, Christian school teachers—basically any number of positions that involve some aspect of teaching.

Both men and women selected family, friends, and pastoral staff as the major contributors to their coming to Christ. Men mentioned friends more often than women (19.3 percent compared to 12.3 percent), but pastoral staff had more direct influence than friends in the lives of women (16.5 percent to 12.3 percent; see graph below).

The Person Who Led Men and Women to Faith in Christ

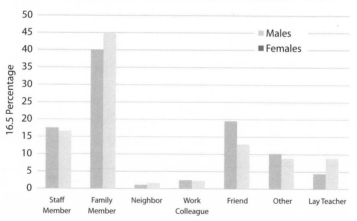

For this study, new converts were defined as persons who had recently received Christ as their Savior and were not attending a church prior to the one in which they completed the survey. Among new converts to Christ, family was noted most often (31.8 percent) as the person who brought them to faith in Christ, while friends and staff were mentioned equally (22.7 percent). It's interesting that no new believers indicated that a teacher led them to Christ. Certainly a number of reasons could be given to account for this, but perhaps the simplest is that they would not have been involved in a class or group led by a teacher (see graph below).

The Person Who Led New Convert to Faith in Christ

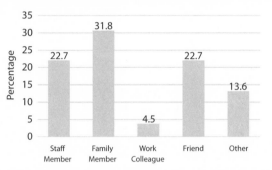

In contrast to new converts, church transfers were less influenced by friends (14.7 percent versus 22.7 percent) and pastoral staff (16.4 percent versus 22.7 percent) but more influenced by teachers (9.7 percent versus 0.0 percent of new converts) (see graph below). Church transfers differ from new converts due to the fact that they had accepted Christ more than two years before the survey and had attended a church before the one in which they took the survey.

The survey asked people to self-identify as a Builder (born before 1945), a Boomer (born between 1946 and 1964), a GenXer (born between 1965 and 1984), or a Millennial (born after 1984). Builders give more credit to teachers for their coming to Christ (11.7 percent) than any other age group, which may be related to the important evangelistic role that

The Person Who Led Church Transfer to Faith in Christ

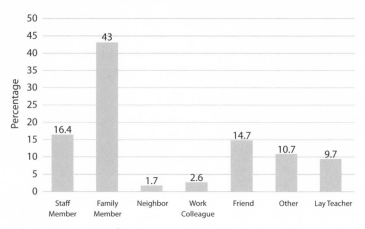

Sunday school teachers played in prior years. Friends were more crucial to Boomers (17.4 percent) and GenXers (16.8 percent) than either Builders (8.9 percent) or Millennials (14.3 percent). There appears to be a declining impact of pastoral staff and teachers on the younger generations but an increased importance (except for Boomers) of family (see graph below).

The Person Who Led Each Generation to Faith in Christ

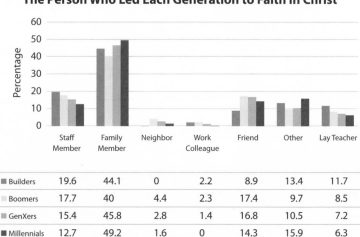

	Staff Member	Family Member	Neighbor	Work Colleague	Friend	Other	Lay Teacher
Builders	19.6	44.1	0	2.2	8.9	13.4	11.7
Boomers	17.7	40	4.4	2.3	17.4	9.7	8.5
GenXers	15.4	45.8	2.8	1.4	16.8	10.5	7.2
Millennials	12.7	49.2	1.6	0	14.3	15.9	6.3

Six categories of community were analyzed: rural (population less than 10,000), small town (10,000–25,000), small city (25,000–100,000), medium city (100,000–500,000), large city (500,000–1 million), and metropolis (more than 1 million).

While there are a couple of exceptions, the smaller the community, the more important a staff member's role is in leading people to faith. This is likely due to the more relational nature of ministry in smaller communities. Pastors in settings with less population typically spend more time in direct pastoral care, which builds deep relationships, often leading to faith decisions. In contrast, pastors serving in communities with a larger population base commonly focus on organizational details, while leaving pastoral care

The Person Who Led You to Faith in Christ by Region

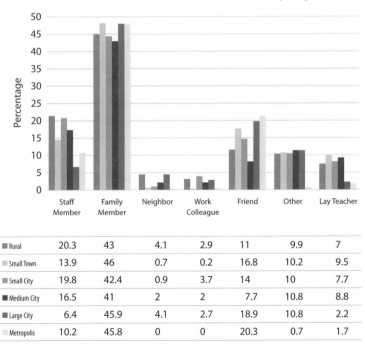

	Staff Member	Family Member	Neighbor	Work Colleague	Friend	Other	Lay Teacher
■ Rural	20.3	43	4.1	2.9	11	9.9	7
■ Small Town	13.9	46	0.7	0.2	16.8	10.2	9.5
■ Small City	19.8	42.4	0.9	3.7	14	10	7.7
■ Medium City	16.5	41	2	2	7.7	10.8	8.8
■ Large City	6.4	45.9	4.1	2.7	18.9	10.8	2.2
■ Metropolis	10.2	45.8	0	0	20.3	0.7	1.7

to others. The role of friends takes on greater importance for people living in larger cities and metropolitan areas (see graph above).

Those responding "other" to questions in the study were referring to a diverse group of people who had brought them to faith. A sampling of people mentioned included evangelists and television preachers like Billy Graham, Pat Robertson, and Charles Stanley, a member of the Gideons, and college or high school campus leaders. None of these, however, were mentioned enough times to be significant to this study. Several responders could not identify any person as a direct influence on their becoming a Christian. They pointed to an inner conviction from God, the Holy Spirit, reading the Bible, or personal experience whereby they accepted Christ in a private manner.

The insight that most people come to faith in Christ through family and friends is not new. There are plenty of illustrations in the Bible of people coming to faith through relational bridges. For example, the apostle John told the story of Andrew. He was listening to John the Baptist, his teacher, who introduced him to Jesus. After spending some time with Jesus, Andrew then "found first his own brother Simon" and "brought him to Jesus" (John 1:41–42). The following day Jesus met Philip in what at first appeared to be a chance encounter, but Philip was from "Bethsaida, of the city of Andrew and Peter" (v. 44), so there may have been a friendship connection. Then Philip found his friend Nathanael and introduced him to Jesus (vv. 45–51). The family and friendship connections are unmistakable.

Likewise, Cornelius was instrumental in helping to bring his family and associates to faith by gathering them to hear the apostle Peter. At first Peter was quite reluctant to speak to Gentiles, but following a divine message given to him through a vision, he changed his thinking. When he arrived at Cornelius's home, he found all of "his relatives and close friends" gathered to hear the gospel (Acts 10:24). Peter then witnessed to the life, death, and resurrection of Jesus (vv. 39–40), and everyone in Cornelius's network of family and friends believed (vv. 44–48).

Paul's ministry of evangelism and church planting was also empowered through the family and friends of those to whom he preached. Lydia's whole household believed and was baptized (16:14–15), as were the Philippian jailer's network (vv. 31–33).

Down-to-Earth Ideas

Putting the insights found in this chapter and the Bible to use will dramatically increase a church's evangelism effectiveness. The following ideas will help this to happen right away.

1. Encourage people in your church to focus on reaching members of their own family for Christ.
2. Strategize how to use the friendship networks of your people for evangelism.
3. Include evangelism as a major ingredient of pastoral care.
4. Inspire teachers in all church-related ministries to share the gospel of salvation and call for decisions.
5. Help your people write out their own testimonies. You may wish to use Acts 26 as a model. When individuals are prepared to share their own story, it is amazing to see how God opens doors for them to do so.

6. Have one or two individuals each month share their testimonies during a worship service. This will encourage both the ones who share and those who hear.

7. Equip your people to share the gospel by using *Becoming a Contagious Christian* (Bill Hybels and Mark Mittelberg) or *Oikos, Your World, Delivered* (Tom Mercer) or *8 to 15: The World Is Smaller Than You Think* (Tom Mercer). For example, involve your people in a small-group, in-home, evangelistic Bible study. Home Bible studies are an effective way to reach people with the gospel. One such study is *Discovering the Lord* by Gordon Penfold.[6]

What person led you to faith in Christ? How about others in your network of friends and family? Who led them to faith? Why not explore this question with others this week and see what you discover?

8

What Method Most Influenced Your Decision for Christ?

"So what's new in your life, Bob?" Mike asked as the two of them stepped out of his car.

"The same as usual," Bob responded with his typical short reply.

"Is that good or bad? 'The usual,' I mean," Mike continued as they walked into the coffee shop.

"Mostly good, I'd say." Bob grinned as he sat down in their regular corner booth and started looking at the breakfast menu. "Which reminds me. I've been meaning to ask you a question."

"Ask away," Mike encouraged.

"Well, our small group is doing some research for the pastor. He wants to find out what particular program or ministry of our church is most effective."

"Okay. So what does he mean by effective?" Mike asked.

"He wants to know which of our programs are most effective in bringing people to faith in Christ," Bob replied. "For me, it was several long conversations with the associate pastor. My wife says it was her attendance at Sunday school when she was a child. What about you and Mary? Can you think of any special program or ministry that influenced your coming to faith?"

"My first thought is the premarital counseling class we attended at church before we got married. Mary was already a believer in Christ, but I wasn't. The couple that taught the class talked about how marriages last longer when people have the same faith. Over the eight sessions, they shared the Christian gospel, and it slowly began to make sense to me. At the last class they asked those of us who wished to accept Christ to pray with them. I prayed that day. So I guess it was that class and, of course, the teachers."

"How about Mary?" Bob probed. "You said she was already a believer. Do you know what influenced her to faith?"

"Yep. I've heard her story over and over. She grew up in a broken family that never went to church. Then when her older brother went to college, he met some campus leaders who were Christians. At first he was a bit cautious, but by his junior year, he made a commitment to Christ at a Christmas conference sponsored by the campus ministry."

"That's cool!" Bob smiled as Mike drank some coffee.

Mike put down his cup and continued his story. "As I recall Mary's story, her brother came home during the university's January break and started sharing about his new experience of faith. Mary was really intrigued. They talked off and on about Christ for the next three weeks. Before her brother went back to school for his spring semester, he asked her if she'd like to pray to receive Christ, and she did. That's the story as I remember it. But you can ask her to tell you more next week when we get together for dinner."

"I will," Bob agreed. "I'm going to be asking several of our friends at church the same question."

Mike and Bob's brief conversation focuses on a key question: What method influenced you to come to faith in Jesus Christ? People answering Arn's original study three decades ago listed the following five major methods: Sunday school (4–5 percent), visitation (1–2 percent), evangelistic crusades (.25–.5 percent), general church programs (2–3 percent), and special programs related to meeting needs (2–3 percent). My new study found eleven methods (see graph below).

What Method Most Influenced Your Decision for Christ?

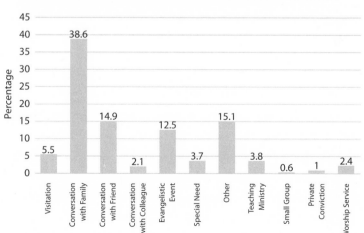

Conversation Is King

Survey responders selected conversation with a family member (38.6 percent) as the main method that brought them to faith in Christ. This corresponds well with the earlier finding that family connections are most responsible for bringing others to faith. Leaving out the category "Other" for the moment, the second highest rated method was conversation with a friend (14.9 percent). While not registering as high a percentage of responses, conversation with a work colleague was chosen 2.1 percent of the time. Together these three responses comprise just over 55 percent of the total responses (55.6 percent). Evidently the best method for leading others to faith in Christ is simply to enter into conversations with them about spiritual things.

Evangelistic crusades, revivals, and special events were chosen by 12.5 percent of the participants, which is much higher than Arn found (0.5 percent). The difference may be related to the way the question was worded. In Arn's original study, the issues of *what person* and *what method* were instrumental in a person's decision for Christ were combined in one question, while they were two different questions in my research. Also, this study combined evangelistic crusades with special events, which may have led to an increase in the number of people marking this option. Whatever the reason for the increase, evangelistic events appear to be a significantly more effective methodology in use today.

Teaching ministry was acknowledged 3.8 percent of the time, which is essentially the same as Arn's earlier finding of 4–5 percent. The low level of impact from educational programs on evangelism over the last few decades may be due to the fact that educational programs tend to emphasize learning rather than evangelism. The same is likely true of small groups, an option chosen less than 1 percent of the time as a method for bringing people to faith. Small groups, as used in the United States, tend to stress Bible study or pastoral care rather than evangelism, although some churches do find fruitfulness using evangelistic Bible studies. Special needs programming was selected twice as often as it was several years ago (3.7 percent, compared to 2 percent). Another method that has become more effective for evangelism is a visit by someone from the church. However, the Arn study was testing *cold* calling, while this study tested *warm* calling, that is, a home visit following a person's first attendance at the church. Thus the two are not identical. Cold calls are not a fruitful methodology for reaching people for Christ, whereas using visitation as a follow-up strategy is helpful in some situations.

Males and females closely mirrored each other's answers, except in two categories (see graph below). Females were slightly more influenced by conversation with family members, while friends swayed males a little more.

What Method Influenced Your Decision for Christ? (Male and Female)

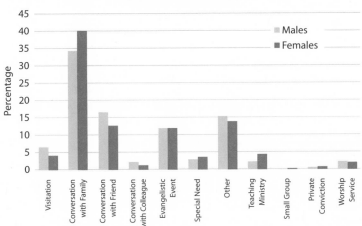

Conversing with members of one's family is a constant for all generations but is somewhat more important to the GenXers and the Millennials. Evangelistic events were more helpful in reaching Millennials than they were for the other three generations surveyed, and this category was almost twice as impactful for Millennials than it was for Boomers and GenXers (see graph below).

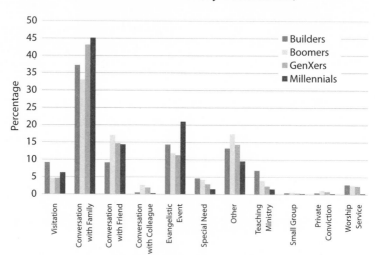

Method of Influence (by Generations)

Conversation with family and friends is the number one method for reaching people for Christ. This method rises in importance when a church is located in a larger community. Evangelistic events are more successful in small communities (see graph below).

Method of Influence (by Region)

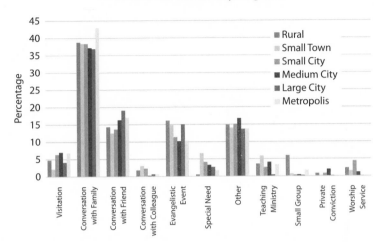

New converts to Christ within the last two years were the only group to select a method other than "Conversation with Family" as the primary method that influenced them for faith in Christ. The combined category of "Other" ranked highest at 27.3 percent (to be discussed later), and "Conversation with Friend," at 22.7 percent, was the next highest (see graph below).

Method of Influence for New Converts

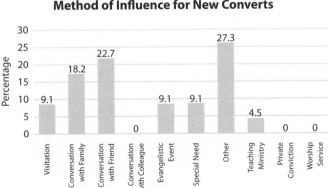

Overwhelmingly, church transfers said they were influenced by conversation with a family member (40.1 percent). Clustered together were two methods that appear to have equal influence on those who moved from another church. Conversation with a friend and evangelistic events were noted about equally (see graph below).

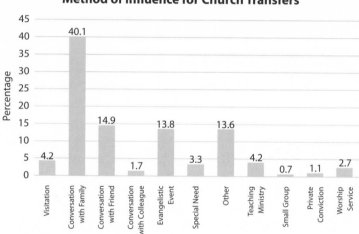

Method of Influence for Church Transfers

Additional Methods

A large number of respondents selected "Other," indicating a method other than those listed as the way they came to Christ. While none of the methods combined in this category were large enough by themselves to show up significantly on the overall survey, they do demonstrate that God employs numerous methods to bring people to faith. The power of a Christian family was recorded as a method for leading children to Christ. Of particular emphasis was regular attendance at church, family devotions, and Bible reading at home. When these are combined with the modeling of a godly life by parents, it is a powerful draw to Christ. Other methods that influenced people for faith were listening to years of consistent sermons from the pastor, personal Bible reading, church camps, Bible studies, and vacation Bible school. Twenty-nine other methods were mentioned, such as TV/radio, campus ministry, a Christmas program, and reading Christian books, but none were noted enough times to be of any significance in the overall study.

Some people were driven to faith in Christ through a "Special Need." New converts selected this method 9.1 percent of the time. In this category, divorce, separation, and remarriage were often mentioned as the need. Close to this was experiencing the death of a friend or close family member. Some said they were driven to faith in Christ due to a deep need to belong and a hunger for the truth. Brokenness also appeared as a major contributor for coming to faith. One person replied, "It was Jesus or suicide." Others mentioned they were on drugs, had suffered abuse as a child, or had been involved in witchcraft. A sense of desperation also caused some to consider Christ, particularly health crises, personal depression, and marital issues.

Comparing these new results with Arn's original study presents a clear picture of how things have changed during the last three decades.

Method	Arn Study	McIntosh Study
Friend/Relative	75–90%	58.9%
Pastor/Staff	5–6%	17.3%
Crusade	0.25–0.5%	12.5%
Visitation	1–2% (cold call)	5.5% (warm call)
Sunday School	4–5%	3.8%
Special Need	1–2%	3.7%
Church Program	2–3%	2.4%
Walk-In	2–3%	<0.25%

Percentages do not add up to precisely 100 percent due to the fact that the results are combined from two different questions. They are correlated here with Arn's original study to show the changes over the past few decades.

Down-to-Earth Ideas

Jesus was a master of conversation. He knew how to ask probing questions that drilled beneath the exterior of surface talk. He carefully listened to what others said, but he also had an ability to understand what was left unsaid. Jesus could talk with anyone from any social, economic, or educational background. Consider his conversations with Nicodemus and the Samaritan woman (John 3 and 4). As an educated man, Nicodemus desired to discuss theology, and Jesus spoke to him about being born again, which was a very esoteric concept. It even confused Nicodemus a bit, and he wondered how a person could go back into his mother's womb to be born again. Then Jesus explained that he was speaking about spiritual things. Later, at a well in Samaria, Jesus met a woman and spoke with her about living water, which was a natural subject for her. Because she had had so little formal education, Jesus spoke to her in a way that made sense. At first, though, she was a little perplexed, not understanding that Jesus was offering the living water of a changed life.

Other examples are easily brought to mind—Jesus speaking with Peter, the woman caught in adultery, and the twelve disciples. He was able to converse with anyone anywhere about spiritual life. Unfortunately the average worshiper in our churches does not seem to know how to enter into conversations about spiritual things with friends, family, colleagues, and, yes, strangers. To train people in your church to be better conversationalists, here are some methods to try.

1. Encourage worshipers to make a list of the people in their networks of family, friends, and colleagues and begin praying for their salvation. Doing so will gradually increase their personal interest in seeing the people on their list come to faith in Christ.

2. Offer listening skills training to people in your church. Start by training 10 percent of your people each year. Not only will this help them converse better with their non-Christian friends, but it will improve communication within your church.

3. Plan church events where your people will feel comfortable bringing their friends, family members, and colleagues. The key is bringing them, not just inviting them. Spiritual conversations take place naturally when Christians are with non-Christians. When people bring some of the people on their prayer lists, they will have time to talk before and after the event.

4. Organize open space in your church building to facilitate conversation. Set up chairs and sofas, along with area rugs, tables, and lamps in several places around your campus. These spaces will quickly fill up with people gathered in conversation, and some of the conversations will get around to spiritual matters.

5. Move the meet-and-greet time from the beginning of your worship service to the end of the service. Conversations that are started while people shake hands are interrupted at the beginning of the worship time as people return to singing. However, when conversations begin

after the worship service, they will often be carried on through the lobby, into the parking lot, and sometimes even into restaurants and homes.

6. Schedule one evangelistic event each quarter in the year. Not only do such events influence some to faith in Christ (12.5 percent), but they also provide members and attendees a place to bring people in their networks. Be sure to provide a clear explanation of the gospel of salvation and give participants an opportunity to make a faith commitment.

7. At least once a month, weave the gospel message into the sermon and follow up by asking those in attendance at worship to make a faith commitment to Christ. Offer the opportunity to meet with the pastor or another staff person to discuss questions with anyone who is interested in receiving Christ as their Savior.

9

Why Did You Begin to Attend Church?

"Before we get started on our Bible study," Mark began at his Thursday night small-group meeting, "the pastor wants me to ask everyone a question. Pastor Dennis is doing some research to find out why people are coming to our church."

Jumping right into the conversation, Shirley offered, "That's an easy question for me to answer. It was the style of the worship service and music. My husband and I wanted a more upbeat worship experience and we heard The Rock Church had a great one."

"Okay, that's a good start. Does anyone else have a reason they'd like to share?" Mark encouraged others in the group to respond.

"Judy and I didn't know anything about this church," Don explained. "Judy was in a carpool that drove by the church five days a week and she suggested we visit. The greeter and people were so warm, we kept coming back."

"I found the church on the internet," Kathy shared. "After listening to a couple of the pastor's messages on the church's website, I was hooked. So I'd say the reason I attended was the pastor. He's just so authentic."

"Let me see," Mark interrupted. "So far, I've written down style of worship service, drive-by, church website, and the pastor's messages. Does that sound right?"

"Sounds right to me," Don agreed, "but *you* haven't said anything. What caused you to attend our church?"

What would you say? What caused you to attend your church? Most people tend to answer this question in one of two ways. They either point to a person or some nonpersonal connection.

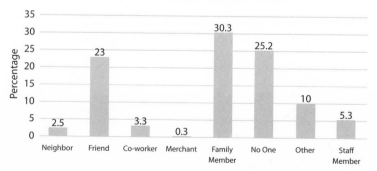

Who Influenced You to Attend Church?

For those who say it was a person, once again friends and family members rank the highest, mentioned by 53.3 percent of people (see graph above). The top five family members who influenced people to attend church were, in order: parents, spouses, children, siblings, and extended family members (for example, cousins, aunts, uncles, grandparents, nieces, and nephews).

Twenty-five percent of people say they just came on their own. When combined with "Other," a full 35 percent of people say they originally connected to church by means other than invitations. The culture of the United States offers numerous ways to connect with a church other than being invited by a friend or family member. Looking back on their initial contact with their church, people mention they just came on their own initiative—what most refer to as walk-ins. We must ask, though, what led them to walk in? People remember driving by and seeing the church building, listening to the pastor on television or radio, seeing the church's website on the internet, or looking for a church in the telephone Yellow Pages. Once they visited, people indicate they chose to continue coming because of the guest welcome and follow-up, the church's position on the Bible, and the friendliness and warmth of the people.

Just under one-third of men say they came to church on their own (No One—29.1 percent), which is exactly the same number of those who say family influenced them (29.1 percent). Less than one-fourth of women (22.8 percent) just walked in, while 31.6 percent originally attended because of an invitation from a family member (see graph below).

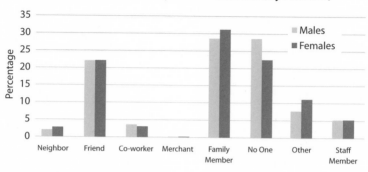

For the Millennial generation, an invitation by a family member is the crucial reason many began to attend church (57.1 percent). This reason is nearly twice as important for Millennials as for the other three generations. Members of the Boomer and GenX generations are also open to the invitations of friends (see graph below).

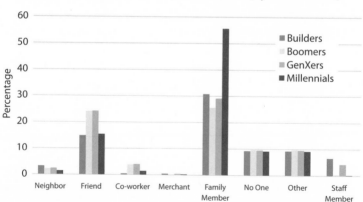

Churches in larger communities typically find more people just walking into the church's worship service without any prior connection to members or worshipers. Except for the large city category, family and friends are strong in all communities, regardless of size (see graph below).

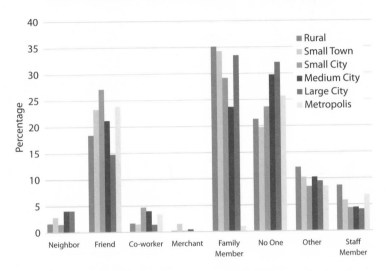

Who Influenced You to Attend Church? (by Region)

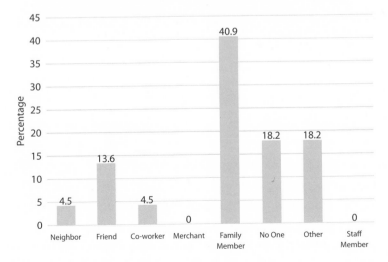

Who Influenced You to Attend Church? (New Converts)

New converts did not indicate any influence from staff members or local merchants as a cause for their attending church. The highest influence was family (40.9 percent), but significantly, the two areas of "Other" and "No One" scored 36.4 percent. Friends were mentioned 13.6 percent of the time (see graph above).

Church transfers are also strongly influenced by family (28.9 percent) and their own choices (indicated by 27.7 percent in the "No One" category). Invitations by friends also rank high at 22.4 percent. Again, it is surprising to find that the two categories of "No One" and "Other" rank so high, with a combined total of 37.7 percent (see graph below).

Who Influenced You to Attend Church? (Church Transfers)

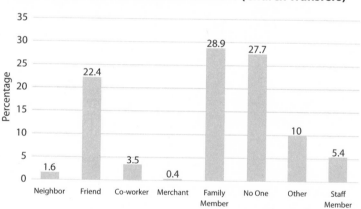

For those who did not indicate a specific person as originally influencing their attendance at church, the following were the top five reasons in order given for attending: preaching of the pastor, theological position of the church, style of the music and worship service, availability of age-group programs, and Sunday school. Responses from new converts who had not previously been involved in any church were slightly different, in the following order: theological position of the church, style of music and worship, preaching of the pastor, the attendance of family, and the availability of small groups.

The location of the church's physical facilities played some part in a person's decision to attend. A little more than half (50.6 percent) said the location had no effect, but 29.2 percent said it did, while 20.1 percent marked "somewhat" (see graph below). Assuming those who said "somewhat" were actually influenced by the church's location, the results are evenly split.

Did the Location of the Church Influence Your Decision to Attend?

This assumption is supported by the fact that 91 percent of people live within twenty miles of the church they attend (see graph below).

Miles Driven to Church

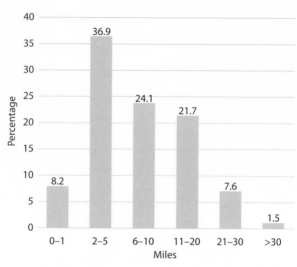

Miles from Church (New Converts)

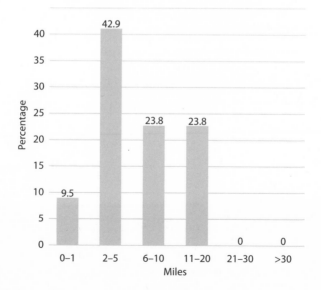

The significance of location is even more pronounced when it comes to those who are new converts to the faith. None of the new converts live farther than twenty miles from the church they attend (see graph above). In fact, 52.4 percent live less than five miles away from church, and 76.2 percent live less than ten miles away.

Theological Beliefs

A church's theological beliefs rank high in importance as a reason for people selecting a new church when they already have a church background (see graph below). A total of 93.3 percent of church transfers indicate that the theology of the new church was highly important, while only 3.6 percent say it was not a factor, and 3.1 percent are uncertain.

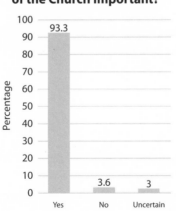

Were the Theological Beliefs of the Church Important?

The theological position of a church is not as important a factor for new converts (see graph below). Only 57.1 percent of new converts said the church's theological position was important, with 14.3 percent saying it was not a factor, and 28.6 percent being uncertain. Since new converts are often not schooled in theology, this is not surprising.

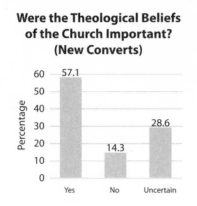

Were the Theological Beliefs of the Church Important? (New Converts)

When the importance of a church's theological position is looked at generationally, it is clear that the youngest generation has slightly less interest than other generations (see graph below).

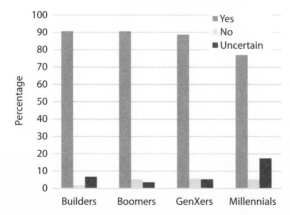

Were the Theological Beliefs of the Church Important? (by Generations)

Just over three-fourths (76.8 percent) of the respondents were regularly attending a church before coming to the one where they completed the survey, while 22.3 percent had not been attending any church (see graph below).

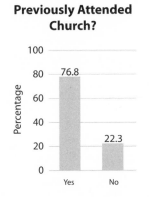

Previously Attended Church?

Of the respondents who had attended church just prior to coming to their new one, one-third had done so due to a recent relocation. However, a little more than one-fourth sought a new style of ministry or new type of ministry, which their previous church did not offer (see graph below). Assuming that those who change jobs also moved, nearly half (44.9 percent) changed churches due to some recent relocation. Two issues were listed enough times as "other" to be included in the figure: doctrinal issues and desired new ministry.

As one can see, numerous factors sway a person to select a church. By empowering current attendees to reach their social networks residing within your church's ministry area, you will increase your church's potential for attracting new attendees.

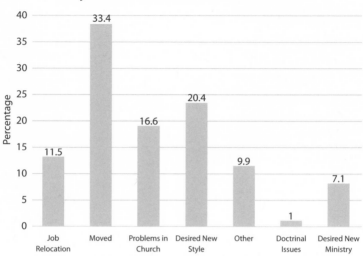

Why Did You Leave Your Previous Church?

Down-to-Earth Ideas

Here are some ideas for methods that can increase the number of visitors at your church.

1. Encourage current church attendees to invite their family and friends to church and appropriate church events. It is wise for churches to offer events specifically for new people to attend. Often labeled seeker events, such gatherings focus on making newcomers welcome and provide a place for them to taste and see that the Lord is good.

2. Clearly communicate to church members and attendees that upcoming sermon series or special events are targeted to new people. Your church members and attendees may be unsure of when is a good time to invite family and friends. Usually they invite others just at Easter, Christmas, or for special events. By telling them that an upcoming event is specifically designed

for newcomers, it will alert them to consider bringing friends and family.

3. Recognize that one-third of people visit a church on their own without anyone guiding them. Church leaders should look at the church facility through guests' eyes and improve the curb appeal for those driving by. Also make certain the church has a working website and increase the church's visibility through advertising. This is particularly important for churches in larger communities, although churches in smaller towns can make a major impact as well with good advertising of a church's program.

4. Study the needs and interests of the Millennial generation (people born after 1984) and then offer events that will meet their felt needs. Since this generation is most responsive to attending church because of family connections, focus on training your own members and attendees to invite them.

5. Highlight the theological positions and values of the church. Both church transfers and new converts (although theology is often not as important to them) indicate that the church's theological position was an important part of their decision to attend. While churches may have played down their theology over the past few decades, those attending churches in today's environment desire to know what a church believes.

6. Be aware that the church's physical location determines a ministry area. Most churches' ministries should consider as a determining parameter the fact that 91 percent of all attendees, and a full 100 percent of new converts, live less than twenty miles from the church they attend.

It is wise for a church's programs, advertising, evange-listic outreaches, and other ministries to target those within a twenty-mile radius.

7. Focus some ministry toward those who have recently moved into your church's ministry area. Since nearly half of all the survey respondents came to their church following a relocation, this indicates that new arrivals are a receptive group whom you should reach. Consider various ways to connect with newcomers in your area, such as welcome bags distributed to new residents.

10

Why Do You Remain at Your Church?

"Our discussion last week on what or who influenced us to first attend church was extremely enlightening." Mark was opening his small-group discussion. "Tonight I'd like to redirect that discussion and ask, what or who influenced you to remain at church? I know there were factors that kept me at church other than those that brought me in the first place. For example, my wife's parents invited us to church, and when we got here, we were overwhelmed by the friendliness of the people. I feel that it was the warm welcome that influenced us to stay. How about you? What caused you to remain at our church?"

After a bit of hesitation, Don spoke up. "The friendliness of the church people was a key factor, but I'd say it was more about the pastor's authenticity. You know, Judy and I felt he was honestly living out what he preached. To us that was more crucial than just the warmth of the congregation."

"Believe it or not," Shirley burst in, "my husband and I found the church name helpful. I grew up in a Baptist church, and Bob attended a Presbyterian church all of his childhood and into his teens. When we discovered The Rock Church, it meant a great deal to us because we have found Jesus to be our Rock. We just love that name and the meaning behind it."

"I agree that the name is a unique one," Kathy offered, "but for me it came down to two things. First, the pastor's conviction as he preaches, and second, the way he applies God's Word to my life. I've never been in a church where the Bible has come so alive."

"Okay," Mark summarized, "what caused us to stay in this church is the church's friendliness and warmth; the pastor's authenticity, conviction, and ability to apply the Bible to our lives; and our unique name, or rather the meaning behind the name. So what do the rest of you think influenced your desire to remain in church?"

While the conversation above is fictitious, it does represent discussions found in numerous churches. The truth is that what influenced us to remain in a church may be quite different from what initially led us to attend.

Friendliness of a Congregation

For many church attendees, the main reason they stay in a church is related in one way or another to the friendliness of the congregation, described as warmth, openness, or acceptance. No one remains at a church for long if it is not invitingly friendly (see graph below). Of all the people responding to this survey, 82.6 percent said the friendliness of the church was a major factor in their decision to stay beyond the first visit. However, 17.4 percent said it was not a factor or that they were uncertain if it was a factor.

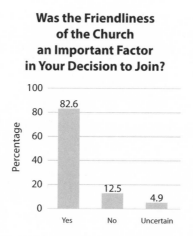

New converts were slightly less impacted by the friendliness of the congregation, with only 72.7 percent saying it was an important aspect of their decision to stay at the church. Note that more than one-fourth (27.3 percent percent) said friendliness was not a factor or they were uncertain of its influence (see graph below).

Importance of Church's Friendliness to New Converts

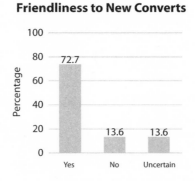

Overall, the friendliness of a church is significant for about four-fifths of all people, but it is vitally important for those living in large cities with between five hundred thousand and one million inhabitants. For cities larger than one million people, the friendliness of a congregation is slightly less influential in helping newcomers remain in the church (see graph below).

Importance of Church's Friendliness (by Region)

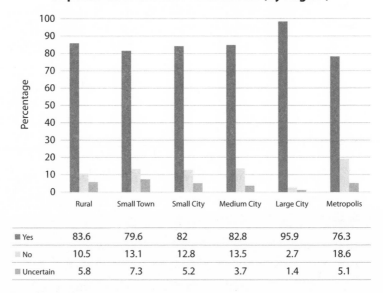

	Rural	Small Town	Small City	Medium City	Large City	Metropolis
Yes	83.6	79.6	82	82.8	95.9	76.3
No	10.5	13.1	12.8	13.5	2.7	18.6
Uncertain	5.8	7.3	5.2	3.7	1.4	5.1

It is vital to note that the importance of a friendly church increases for younger generations. Members of the Builder generation rated the influence of a church's friendliness at 75.7 percent, while members of the Millennial generation rated it at 90.5 percent, an increase of nearly 15 percent in importance (see graph below).

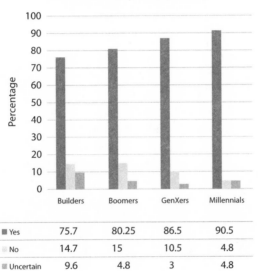

Importance of Church's Friendliness (by Generation)

	Builders	Boomers	GenXers	Millennials
■ Yes	75.7	80.25	86.5	90.5
No	14.7	15	10.5	4.8
▦ Uncertain	9.6	4.8	3	4.8

The Church's Name

Over the past few decades it has been quite popular to rename churches in an effort to attract new people, but based on this research, the name does not appear to have been a major factor in people choosing to attend or stay at a church (see graph below). It should be noted that the survey was not able to question those who had chosen not to stay at the church.

The survey only questioned people who had remained, and the name was clearly not a major factor.

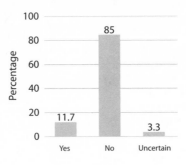

Was the Name of the Church Important?

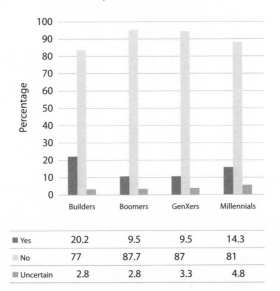

Importance of Church's Name (by Generation)

	Builders	Boomers	GenXers	Millennials
Yes	20.2	9.5	9.5	14.3
No	77	87.7	87	81
Uncertain	2.8	2.8	3.3	4.8

Members of the Builder and Millennial generations (see graph above) seemed more influenced by the church's name than others. One-fifth of the Builder generation found the name of their church a factor in deciding to stay, while nearly 15 percent of the Millennials found it significant. Regardless of this, the graph illustrates that most members of all four generations did not feel the name of their church mattered much in their decision to attend or stay.

The importance of a church's name changes little by region but seems slightly more significant for those located in smaller towns (see graph below).

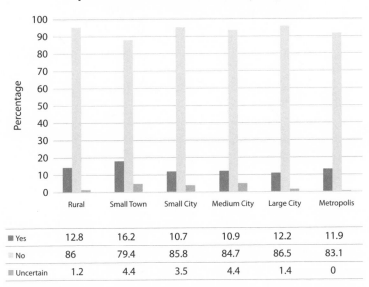

Importance of Church's Name (by Region)

	Rural	Small Town	Small City	Medium City	Large City	Metropolis
■ Yes	12.8	16.2	10.7	10.9	12.2	11.9
■ No	86	79.4	85.8	84.7	86.5	83.1
■ Uncertain	1.2	4.4	3.5	4.4	1.4	0

There is very little difference between church transfers and new converts when it comes to the importance of a church's name (see graph below). The slight difference may be attributed to the reality that church transfers might be looking for a particular church by name, whereas new converts may not. Yet it is interesting that new converts did not find the name important when deciding to remain at a church.

Importance of Church's Name (New Converts and Transfers)

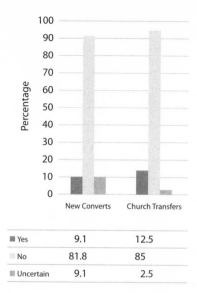

	New Converts	Church Transfers
■ Yes	9.1	12.5
No	81.8	85
■ Uncertain	9.1	2.5

Orientation Class

Some studies have found that a new members class is a significant way to help people stay in a church.[1] The study reported here found that 75.4 percent of churches do offer such an orientation class, but less than half require it for those seeking involvement in the church (see graph below).

Unfortunately 30 percent of new converts were uncertain if their church even offered such a class, and 10 percent of the churches did not have such a class available. Thus a full 40 percent of new converts had no opportunity to attend a new members class. On the other hand, church transfers are more aware of the opportunity to attend a new members class with just 17.3 percent being uncertain of the availability of such a class.

Since studies have shown that people who attend an orientation or new members class are more committed, give more financially, and generally participate more fully in the church's activities, churches need to do a better job of communicating the offering of such a class and should expect or even require new members to attend it.

Did the Church Require Attendance at a New Members Class?

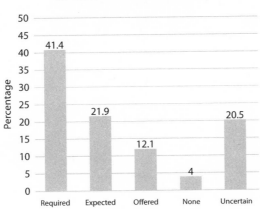

Six Key Factors

Other factors that influenced newcomers to remain in their church were as follows (listed in descending order of importance). Together these six reasons were mentioned by 85 percent of all respondents.

1. The church had a clear mission and vision.
2. The style of the worship service.

3. I gained a clearer understanding of Christian beliefs and teaching.

4. The church had a Sunday school or church school.

5. The church had a place for me to serve.

6. The church had small groups.

The four different generations had slightly different perspectives, but the top three selections were always the church's clear vision and mission, the style of the worship service, and gaining a clearer understanding of Christian beliefs and teaching (see chart below). The numbers indicate how the factor was ranked by those in a particular generation. For example, Mission and Vision was ranked third in importance by Millennials.

Generation	Millennials	GenXers	Boomers	Builders
Mission and Vision	3	1	2	1
Style of Worship Service	1	2	1	3
Beliefs and Teachings	2	3	3	2
Sunday School	6	4	4	4
Place to Serve	4	5	5	5
Small Groups	5	6	6	6

Recent converts and church transfers ranked the six factors slightly differently (see chart below). But the top three factors were the same for them as for the generations.

Category	New Converts	Church Transfers
Mission and Vision	3	1
Style of Worship Service	2	2
Beliefs and Teaching	1	3
Sunday School	5	4
Place to Serve	6	5
Small Groups	4	6

These six factors point to two primary areas of ministry that influenced attendees to remain at the church: (1) the worship service and (2) the connecting ministries of the church. The first three areas, which almost always were chosen first, second, or third, relate in one way or another to the church's worship service. People tend to remain in churches where they relate to the style of worship, which includes the music, atmosphere, and overall experience of worship. This experience includes the clear teaching of the Bible, which is a major aspect of every pastor's ministry. People tend to stay in churches where they hear the Word of God taught in a practical, understandable manner. And while there are many ways that a church's mission and vision are communicated, without question the worship service of a church is a primary way of sharing this pertinent information with the entire congregation. A pastor's ability to communicate is also important, as suggested by the research, and will be discussed in the next chapter.

As is commonly stressed, churches have only one chance to make a first impression, so this point is crucial when it comes to newcomers. What people noticed when first attending a church was the friendly attitude of the congregation. This was variously expressed as warm, loving, open, accepting, caring, inviting, and welcoming. Regardless of how it was expressed, it points to a receptive and comfortable experience for the newcomer. New people also noticed the uplifting atmosphere of the church. This was most often described as "the Lord was there," great teaching and preaching, outstanding worship, and a vibrant and active congregation. What may be of equal importance was that those who remained in the church found that their continued attendance confirmed their first impressions. The longer they attended the church, the more they discovered that their first impression was correct. Indeed over the long run, people stay in a church primarily because they sense they are growing spiritually and in their personal lives. Having a growing connection with others in the congregation (fellowship) is also a main reason people continue attending a church.

The other area of importance was reflected in the three factors related to the newcomer's ability to connect with others in the church. The need to find a place to belong is seen in the selection of Sunday school and small groups, and the importance of being valued is seen in the selection of a place to serve. It has long been known that the three keys to keeping new people in church relates to making friends, having a place to belong, and finding a place to serve. The fourth, fifth, and sixth choices in the chart above are where these things happen for most newcomers. Indeed, this study found that 91.3 percent of all those who stayed in a church were attending a Sunday school class, a small group, a Bible study, or some other sort of group (for example, sports, crafts, discussion, youth group). Unfortunately only 50.3 percent were also involved in some sort of ministry, which seems to indicate it is easier to get people involved in classes and groups than in actual ministry. New converts were slightly more involved at 52.4 percent, indicating they were serving in a role, a task, or job at church.

Down-to-Earth Ideas

As one might expect, the reasons people first attend a church differ somewhat from the reasons they remain. The original impact of the first visit is powerful, with those experiencing a warm and vibrant welcome being most likely to return for subsequent visits. As newcomers become connected in the church at deeper levels of fellowship, service, and participation, the probability they will remain in the church increases. Thus church leaders should consider implementing some of the following ideas to encourage new people to continue in the church for many years to come.

1. Be sure that there is an open and welcoming spirit in the church toward all guests. This takes verbal encouragement from leaders, of course, but will not happen in the majority of churches unless it is accompanied by a strategic plan. For example, it will serve the church well to place the regular welcoming time at the end of the worship service rather than at the beginning. Doing so allows conversations to carry on longer instead of being cut short by the ongoing worship service. It also helps to use a well-organized welcoming system that begins when guests arrive in the parking lot and continues with them into the church and back to their cars later on.

2. Notch up the quality of all aspects of the worship service, including the pastor's sermon, music, lighting, sounds, and supportive services, such as the nursery, other child care, greeting ministry, ushers, signage, and any other aspect of ministry that impacts the atmosphere before, during, and following the worship service.

3. Clearly communicate some part of the church's mission and vision each and every week. Newcomers are drawn to churches that know where they are going and communicate that direction well. Among other possibilities, this should include some mention of the vision

and mission in every sermon or communication from the pulpit. Highlights of the mission and vision should grace the walls, publications, and advertisement in different ways.

4. The style of the worship service should reflect the culture of the people the church is seeking to reach with the gospel. The worship team should reflect the age makeup found in the church's community, and the style of music must be relevant to new people. In all cases, the worship service should cause people to feel uplifted and ready to face the challenges of the coming week.

5. All preaching and teaching should include clarity of application to those in the congregation. Pastors and other speakers must carefully craft each message to fit the felt needs of the congregation, applying the truth of God's Word to the actual lives of the people, that is, to the things the people will face as they return to their homes, work, or school on Monday morning.

6. Make certain that enough classes and small groups are available to connect newcomers with the natural friendship networks of the church. Usually this means a church must have three to seven classes and groups for every one hundred adult attendees at worship.

7. Invite, recruit, train, and place newcomers in places of service as soon as possible, but no later than six months following their first visit to your church. Newcomers are most open to serving during the first half year they attend a church. Since most churches are not comfortable involving newcomers in teaching ministries, a significant number of entry-level positions should be available

within the church. Most churches find that newcomers are best used in the welcoming, greeting, and parking ministries of the church at the start. Then after some observation, they can be moved to other ministries as they prove to be faithful servants.

11

What Is the Pastor's Role in Evangelism?

"Have you heard about the research our pastor has been doing?" Silvia casually inquired as Carol slid into her car.

"Yes. Hasn't everyone?" Carol remarked, buckling her seat belt. "My small group has discussed several questions over the last few months. I've found it very interesting."

"Me too!" Silvia agreed. "But I think we're missing a major factor in how people come to Christ and a church."

"Oh? What's missing?"

"No one is asking what the pastor's role is in all of this," continued Silvia. "The way I see it, the pastor plays a major role in bringing people to faith, as well as into our church."

"For sure. I'd be willing to bet the pastor is most important in getting people to stay after they visit."

"That sounds right," Silvia acknowledged. "I know Phil and I wouldn't attend a church if we didn't like the pastor's preaching."

"Double for sure," Carol exclaimed. "I wonder what others think about the pastor's role in keeping people?"

There is no doubt that pastors are a major part of any church's ministry. Most pastors preach on a regular schedule, work closely with leaders and volunteers, and participate in nearly all decisions that impact a church's ministry. Further, as this study reveals, they are crucial to the process of helping people find faith in Christ and in becoming responsible members of a local church.

As referenced previously, in answer to the question What person was it that led you to come to faith in Christ?, 17.3 percent of recent church members selected a staff member. For new converts, staff members ranked slightly higher, with 22.7 percent choosing this option, while just 16.4 percent of church transfers said it was a staff member (see graphs in chapter 7). Admittedly, not all staff members are lead pastors, so the actual impact of solo or senior pastors on bringing people to faith is likely lower than these staff percentages indicate. Yet pastors (solo or senior) have influence in attracting people to church and/or in keeping them after they come.

Attracting People to Church

When survey respondents were asked, What person was the greatest influence in your attending this church?, only 5.3 percent selected a staff member (see graph below).

What Person Influenced You to Attend Church?

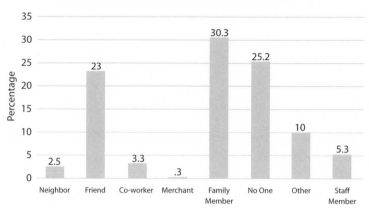

Staff members ranked fifth behind family members (30.3 percent), no one (25.2 percent), friends (23 percent), and other (10 percent) as the reason people *first* attended a church. In growing churches it is common for church attendees to have an average of nine unchurched friends or family members living within the church's ministry area. In plateaued and declining churches, attendees average six unchurched friends and three family members.[1] Pastors average the same numbers, and sometimes even fewer due to the fact that they spend most of their time within the relationship circles of church members. Thus pastors usually rank low as a reason people first choose to attend a church. Even if pastors work to build relationships with those outside a church, they will, like most people, succeed in connecting with perhaps nine to twelve unchurched people. For any church to be effective in winning people to faith in Christ and to connect them to a church, it takes the entire membership and attendees to be actively involved.

Pastors do, of course, play a major role in encouraging regular church attendees to invite and bring those in their social networks. When current church attendees find the overall worship experience uplifting, they are most likely to invite and bring their unchurched family and friends to church. The pastor's preaching is a key part of the overall worship experience in a church.

Keeping People at Church

When it comes to *the reason people remain* in a church, the pastor's role ranks very high. This is clearly seen in the three main reasons people give for staying in a church discussed in chapter 10. Having a clear mission and vision, a celebrative worship experience, and a clear understanding of Christian beliefs and teaching are all directly related to the pastor's role. It is primarily through preaching that mission and vision are communicated to the congregation at large and Christian beliefs are clarified.

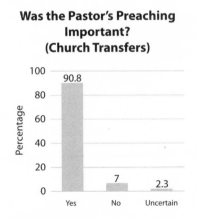

Was the Pastor's Preaching Important? (Church Transfers)

Church transfers place a great deal of importance on how they perceive the pastor's preaching. A total of 90.8 percent of all transfers ranked the pastor's preaching as very important in their decision to attend the church, while just 7 percent said it was not important, and 2.3 percent were uncertain (see graph above).

In contrast, new converts were slightly less impacted by the pastor's preaching, but it still commanded a positive response of 81 percent. New converts were split evenly at 9.5 percent each on the pastor's preaching having no influence and being uncertain if it did or did not affect their decision to attend.

In response to the question, What factors of the pastor's ministry influenced your choice of this church?, the following five factors were chosen by 80 percent of the respondents.

1. Preaching that teaches and applies to my life
2. Authenticity of the pastor
3. Pastor's convictions
4. Pastor's leadership skills
5. Feeling at ease when around the pastor

The selections of new converts to faith in Christ were slightly different, with 80 percent selecting the following top five.

1. Preaching that teaches and applies to my life
2. Authenticity of the pastor
3. Personal contact by the pastor
4. Pastor's sense of humor
5. Pastor's leadership skills

The pastor's preaching, authenticity, and convictions were selected by all generations as critical factors. Members of the Millennial generation placed more importance on the pastor's sense of humor than other generations (see chart below).

Generation	Millennials	GenXers	Boomers	Builders
Pastor's Preaching	1	1	1	1
Pastor's Authenticity	2	3	2	2
Pastor's Convictions	5	2	3	3
Pastor's Leadership		4	4	4
Feeling at Ease around the Pastor	4		5	5
Pastor's Sense of Humor	3	5		

People living in smaller communities placed greater emphasis on feeling at ease around the pastor, while those in larger cities gave higher marks to a pastor's sense of humor. However, respondents from all communities, regardless of size, noted the importance of the following in order: (1) the pastor's preaching, (2) the pastor's authenticity, and (3) the pastor's convictions.

The pastor's influence plays a major part in the process of evangelism. In general, the pastors of smaller churches are the ones who actually lead people to make a commitment to Christ. Members and attendees may bring unbelievers to church, but quite often it is the pastor who guides a person to a faith commitment. Pastors of larger churches play a major role in creating an atmosphere and passion for evangelism, but they often do not personally lead people to faith.

Down-to-Earth Ideas

As we have seen, the pastor of a church can be very influential in drawing people to a church and keeping them there. Here are some ideas that will increase a pastor's effectiveness.

1. Maintain a passion for winning the lost to Jesus Christ. A pastor's convictions seep out in every conversation,

meeting, and teaching/preaching event. Without even knowing it, pastors reveal their underlying passions and convictions about ministry. Thus, if pastors wish to build churches committed to evangelism and outreach, they must be involved in reaching out to nonbelievers themselves.

2. Build relationships with unbelievers and spend at least 10 percent of your time with them outside of church ministries and programs. For example, join an athletic club, become part of a local reading group, coach a team (chess, athletic, debate, for example), or join a civic club such as Rotary or Kiwanis to establish contact with unbelievers.

3. Pray every day for the salvation of people in your immediate family, among your unchurched friends, and in your extended network or associates. If you do not already use one, start making a prayer list in a journal or on your computer or other electronic device. Then pray daily for at least one person on your list.

4. Create casual forums for spiritual conversations, especially for younger adults. Allowing for open questions and answers in a loving environment is a positive way to mentor unbelievers toward acceptance of Christ.

5. Preach regularly on the gospel of salvation and encourage people to believe in Jesus Christ. Focus sermons on God's love and care, the need for personal salvation, insights for personal spiritual growth, and practical advice for daily living. Take care to proclaim the entire canon of Scripture but stress application of all preaching and teaching.

6. Begin a class or small group to train 10 percent of your people each year in friendship evangelism. Find

an evangelistic training program that you like or write your own and then teach it faithfully for a minimum of five years. If you train 10 percent of your people each year for five years, you will have trained half of your people. At that point, the atmosphere of the church will change considerably, as members and attendees are sensitized to caring for nonbelievers.

7. Spend time developing your speaking abilities and sermons. With more than four-fifths of church attendees noting that the pastor's preaching was important to their decision to attend (church transfers 91 percent and new converts 81 percent), this is the place where a pastor has the most control in improving a church's ministry. In addition, churches should provide excerpts or complete messages from the pastor on their website, so that visitors to the site can listen to the pastor speak.

Part 3

Evangelism Today

Principles of
Effective Evangelism

The main methodology that is effective in winning nonbelievers to faith in Christ is simply conversation, which is actually more of a principle than a methodology. In reality methods are short-lived, being, as they are, products of particular times, places, and people. Conversation is a principle, namely, an underlying foundational truth, that works in all times, places, and among all peoples. Conversation is supported by other principles, for example, that relationships are central to communicating the gospel. Conversation always takes place in relationship with another, even if it is a one-way conversation instead of two-way, which is always much better.

With an understanding of the importance of conversation and relationship, other principles of evangelism are offered here. Their use and effectiveness have been observed in fruitful evangelistic churches. In the final analysis, one principle builds on another, with each one enlightening the whole.

Principle 1: Demanded by God

Effective evangelism is demanded by God.

When Jesus commanded his followers to make disciples, he expected them to obey. Sowing the seed of the gospel through presence evangelism activities is just the beginning. Communicating the gospel message through proclamation evangelism methodologies is necessary so people understand the message. The end desire is persuasion evangelism, whereby lifelong disciples are won to faith in Jesus Christ and enfolded into his church. The harvest is ripe, and God expects us to be active in reaping a harvest of souls.

Consider: How involved is your church in each of the three areas of evangelism: sowing the seed, proclaiming the gospel message, and persuasion? Do you think God is pleased with your church's obedience in reaching others with the gospel of salvation? Why or why not?

Principle 2: Measurable

Effective evangelism is measurable.

Wise farmers measure success by the harvest. What matters supremely in the end is not how much energy is spent on preparing the ground or how many hours are spent in sowing the seed or even how much money is spent in cultivating the crop. What matters in the end is the size of the harvest. Similarly, what ultimately matters in evangelism is not how many people have been helped (presence), or how many people have heard (proclamation), but rather how many people have believed in Christ and followed him as his disciple (persuasion).

Consider: How many new disciples has your church made in the last year, the last three years, the last five years? What do the results indicate about your church's obedience to the Great Commission? What do they say about the church's fruitfulness?

Principle 3: Focus on Relationships

Effective evangelism focuses on existing relationships.

There is a direct connection between the number of unchurched friends the adult worshipers of your church have and the potential growth of your church. If your adult attendees average only three unchurched friends, your church is likely to decline. If they have an average of six unchurched friends, your church is probably plateaued. However, if each of the adults in your church has nine or more unchurched friends, your church is very likely to be growing.[1] The more relationships with non-Christians adults have outside of your church, the greater the potential to see people coming to faith in Christ and to your church.

Effective evangelism begins at the basic levels of language, love, and learning. Conversation works best among those who trust each other and share a similar lifestyle. This allows the believer's witness to be examined for integrity and consistency.

Consider: How many redemptive relationships do you have with nonbelievers? How many do the key leaders of your church have? What is the average number of redemptive relationships among attendees? What does this indicate about the church's evangelistic potential?

Principle 4: Intentional

Effective evangelism is intentional.

Even though God is the one who saves, people are needed to persuade nonbelievers of their need of salvation. Normally people do not come to Christ by accident. Instead, God works through faithful churches that plan, strategize, and train their people for evangelism. Left on their own, churches will turn inward, focusing on the people already in attendance instead of reaching out to win new people to Christ. This may be due to our natural tendency toward selfishness or mere neglect of ultimate priorities. No matter the reason, church leaders must work hard to keep evangelism the main thing.

Consider: How intentional is your church in planning, strategizing, and training people for evangelism? What seems to get in the way of intentional evangelism in your church or ministry?

Principle 5: A Balance

Effective evangelism is a balance between truth and relationship.

While relationships are central to any effective evangelistic effort, they must always be balanced with the truth of God's Word. It is certain that loving relationships can go on for some time, even years, without the gospel of salvation being shared. For effective evangelism to occur, the truth about God, Christ, mankind, sin, future judgment, repentance, and personal faith must be part of the conversation within the relationship if people are to believe on Jesus Christ for their salvation.

Consider: Are people in the church engaging in redemptive conversations with their nonbelieving family, friends, and associates? What are the barriers that keep people from talking about their faith with others?

Principle 6: Training in Sharing Faith

Effective evangelism is the result of training believers to share their faith with others.

While it is nice to assume that believers will naturally share their faith out of love for Christ and a deep commitment to his gospel, the fact is most do not do so. Yet when they are trained to do so, church members and worshipers *will* share their faith. As churches train their members to share their faith, around 12 percent of the family members, friends, and colleagues of those trained come to faith in Christ over a five-year period.

Consider: Does your church train members to share their faith? How many people have been trained in the last year, the last three years, the last five years?

Principle 7: Involves Church Activities

Effective evangelism involves nonbelievers in church activities before they believe.

Some people are bold enough to join a new group quickly, but others, perhaps most, prefer to explore new relationships cautiously. Therefore churches that effectively reach others for Christ usually offer several events each year for the sole purpose of connecting nonbelievers to the church *before* they accept Christ. As a rule, churches should schedule a minimum of one event each quarter to meet and connect with the nonbelieving family, friends, and associates of its members.

Consider: Does your church schedule events for the purpose of connecting with nonbelievers? If so, how many events are normally scheduled each year?

Principle 8: Leads to Community

Effective evangelism leads new believers into community.

Christ developed a band of believers who carried on his mission of seeking and saving the lost. Whenever new disciples were made, they were embraced by the community of faith—a local church. This is ultimately what makes evangelism effective, drawing new believers into a church. Then they are able to learn about and from Christ and grow in their faith. The New Testament knows of no independent believers. The church is a gathered community of faith whereby members grow spiritually as they love, care for, and serve one another.

Consider: How well does your church connect with new disciples? What barriers do new believers have to overcome to be accepted and involved in your church? How could you pry open the doors of acceptance so new believers would feel welcomed and be involved within six months of becoming part of your church?

Principle 9: Supported by Prayer

Effective evangelism is supported by prayer.

Prayer is essential for all areas of ministry and perhaps is most crucial for effective evangelism. People who desire results from their evangelism efforts pray for their nonbelieving family members, friends, and associates. They pray for open doors for entering into redemptive conversations, they pray for wisdom to use the right words when conversing about spiritual things, and they pray for the courage to speak up about Jesus Christ at teachable moments.

Consider: Are the members of your church praying evangelistically? Do they pray for the salvation of people in your ministry area? Do they pray passionately for their unbelieving family members, friends, and associates? How about your own prayers? Do you ever pray about evangelism in your private, public, and small-group prayers?

Principle 10: A Process

Disciple making is a process.

Regeneration happens in a moment of time (see John 5:24; Titus 3:5). However, while conversion happens in a moment, the process of coming to faith most often takes place over time, through several events, and in a mysterious manner. New birth is a spiritual experience, undetected by the human eye. We can see the external responses and actions of an individual but not the inner working of his or her heart. Therefore churches that effectively make disciples engage in regular, even routine, practices of evangelism, recognizing that God works in his time and place. It is our responsibility to keep working, keep preaching, and keep training worshipers for evangelism, trusting in God's timing for the salvation of others.

Consider: How faithful are you at continuing the work of evangelism? What tempts you to give up or become lax in your evangelistic efforts? In what ways do you show patient respect for the mysterious working of the Holy Spirit in the lives of others?

Very likely there are other principles for effective evangelism. You may be thinking of some right now. The ones offered here form the basic core of effective evangelism, used by churches that seek to be fruitful in reaching the lost with the gospel of salvation.

Probing Questions

1. Which of the principles of effective evangelism can you identify in your church?
2. Which of the principles are ignored or neglected in your church or ministry?
3. Which one principle will you stress this year?

13

Inviting Others
to Dine with Jesus

The story is an old one but one that needs telling over and over again. Matthew invited his friends to dine with Jesus, and while we know little about the results of that meal, we assume that likely some believed in Jesus and continued to follow him throughout their lives. We know that other similar encounters with Jesus bore the fruit of salvation, and it is reasonable to think Matthew's dinner party did also.

Since you have read this far in *Growing God's Church*, it is reasonable to assume you want to invite others to dine with him. If this assumption is correct, following are a baker's dozen ideas for you to consider using in the coming years.

Strengthening the Effectiveness of Our Invitation

Build a Conscience for Evangelism

What is an evangelistic conscience? It is an attitude that permeates the thinking and the decision-making process of a church. It is an attitude that sees people outside of Christ as lost and rejoices when new people join the church, especially if they are new converts. An evangelistic conscience prioritizes disciple making. It is an attitude that resonates with the Great Commission found in its various forms throughout Scripture.

Evaluate your church's commitment to evangelism and then discuss your evaluation with the church leadership. Are church leaders really committed to the Great Commission of making disciples? If so, how can you tell? Does the church budget confirm your commitment? How about the many ministries your church offers? How many are focused on evangelism in some precise manner?

Review the Mission of Your Church

It is important that a church have a formal statement describing its purpose or mission, and evangelism should be part of that purpose. In response to the formal mission statement, the church's activities, staff, budget, and program should reflect the pursuit of the evangelistic purpose.

Talk with the church board about how to build stronger commitment to evangelism in the church. If you are a pastor, preach on the topics of the Great Commission, evangelism, and the mission of your church. Perhaps a churchwide study on the book of Acts and its implications for your church or study of the topics found in chapters 2 through 6 of this book might be of help in increasing your church's commitment to evangelism.

When people in your church have the attitude that "building friendships with people outside of Christ and our church is part of our Christian commitment," the church is ready to move out in evangelism. As I overheard a person remark in a church, "You can't be around our church for long without bumping into the importance of reaching lost people."

Sponsor Servant Evangelism Activities

Servant evangelism is the practice of sharing Jesus Christ with others through intentional acts of kindness. Servant evangelism activities are simple, fun, and practical ways to connect with the unbelieving community in your church's ministry area, as well as with friends, family, and associates of church members.

Begin by praying for those you will be reaching, as well as for the people in the church who will participate. Then observe the community by prayer walking around neighborhoods or doing a windshield tour—driving around the area. Talk with people in the community and observe the needs, problems, and issues readily apparent, and make a list of practical areas of need the people in your church could address. Then select a few of the items on the list, recruit some people, and leave the church campus to go do them. Here are ten servant evangelism activities other churches have completed in their church communities:

Neighborhood window washing—going door-to-door and offering to wash windows.

Mother's Day flower giveaway—giving away carnations outside a grocery store on the Saturday before Mother's Day.

Snow removal—going door-to-door and offering to shovel sidewalks for free.

Yard cleanup—going door-to-door and offering to clean up yards.

Rainy day grocery escort—holding an umbrella for shoppers as they walk to their cars.

Car wash—washing cars for free.

Smoke detectors—giving out free smoke detectors and batteries.

Laundromat ministry—paying for washing and drying at laundromats.

Leaf raking—offering to rake and dispose of leaves.

Balloon giveaway—giving balloons to kids in a park.

Start small by sponsoring about one servant evangelism event every quarter, and then increase them until you have one per month. Such events offer a low-threat way to involve your people in outreach, and they build solid relationships with people in the community. While these activities do not often win people to Christ, they do start the process of presence evangelism.

Build Relationships

The people of a church need training in building relationships and in identifying unreached family members, friends, and acquaintances.[1] A pastor can preach a sermon series, such as Making Friends for Jesus. During the sermon the pastor can ask the people to make a list of all the friends, family members, and associates they have who are not believers in Jesus Christ and who live within the church's ministry area (a twenty-mile radius). One way to do this is to distribute small cards to those at worship. Then give them about five minutes to write down as many names of people that they can and make a duplicate list. They will turn in one list and keep the other.

Collect the cards and total the number of people listed to see how many connections your people are able to list. While there is no guarantee that unbelieving people on the lists will come to faith in your church, it is a fact that when churches encourage people to build relational bridges with the unchurched, the likelihood of winning new people to faith in Christ increases.

Relationships are the primary way that people come to faith in Christ and to a church. The relationships, however, must be genuine ones; friendships are most effective when they are motivated by love, embrace the hurts and needs of others, and relate authentically in honest discussion.

Pray for the Salvation of People

Encourage a yearlong emphasis on prayer for the salvation of people in your ministry area. Churches that are fruitful in their evangelism efforts make prayer a constant and conscious practice. This is important because prayer is the source of our power for evangelism and can overcome opposition or resistance to the gospel message.

1. Focus on praying in a general way for the salvation of people in the church's ministry area.
2. Focus on praying for those in the social networks of the members and worshipers.
3. Ask God to open doors or opportunities to engage in spiritual conversations.

4. Ask for wisdom in knowing what to say when the opportunities arise.

5. Ask God for the courage to speak when there is an opportunity.

Be sure to encourage people to pray on their own for individuals on their lists.

Design Events for Guests

Design events where people can bring their friends, family, and associates. Well-planned and executed church ministries, events, and programs serve to encourage people of the church to reach out to and invite outsiders.[2] Activities for families, singles, children, youth, and older folks are solid ways to connect with the unchurched person. Sports activities, musical presentations, dramas, and events built around the natural times when people are most likely to attend church—Easter, Mother's Day, Independence Day, Thanksgiving, Christmas—all provide a place for people to test out Christianity before committing to Christ and a church.

Effective evangelism uses strategic events and training. You may not have noticed it, but the New Testament records very few people who came to faith one-on-one. Nicodemus (John 3), the woman at the well (John 4), and Zacchaeus (Luke 19) are several. In contrast to normal thinking, most people appear to have accepted Christ when they were with a group. As noted in the author's study, family, friends, and neighbors are most often credited with bringing people to faith, but it was usually in a group situation that a person made a personal decision for faith. Jesus preached to crowds (Matt. 4:23), and so did Peter (Acts 2). Of course it's not just one way or the other, as God brings people to faith alone and in crowds, but most churches find the most effective evangelistic fruitfulness when the two methods are integrated. Thus helping church attendees connect with their unchurched networks of friends, family, and acquaintances is primary, and providing events to which people may be introduced to the gospel of salvation is part of the process. Think of sponsoring a family fun day, a comedy night, or a Big Sunday or Friend Day event when you seek to fill the church to capacity.

Organize Evangelistic Worship Services

Since guests will usually attend weekend worship services, it is a good idea to organize them around evangelism. No doubt some will ask, "Aren't a church's worship services to be for believers?" The answer is yes, but worship services may also be for unbelievers. All people—believers and unbelievers—face similar life issues. For example, all people struggle with family concerns (rebellious children or poor communication), problems at work or school (dealing with overbearing managers or bullies), broken relationships (disloyal friends or divorce), spiritual questions (untimely deaths or the success of unworthy leaders), as well as financial troubles and managing stress.

Believers and unbelievers struggle with knowing God. It's just that they are at different points in the struggle. Instead of speaking just to long-term believers each weekend, why not intentionally design your services to speak to both believers and unbelievers? For instance, when the pastor delivers the message, it could have three levels of application to challenge everyone in attendance—the unbeliever, the new believer, and the mature Christian. By doing this the same sermon will apply to three different people: a nonbeliever, a new believer, and a long-term believer.

The importance of personal relationships in bringing people to faith in Christ cannot be ignored, but the church as a whole plays a crucial role too. Celebrative worship services led by enthusiastic musicians, warm people, and good teaching are significant support for those bringing unbelievers to church.

Schedule Outreach Ministries

Schedule two or three outreach ministries to target groups in the community. Without exception, churches that effectively reach new people for Christ keep evangelism as a priority. Yes, there are lots of ways to evangelize, and churches may want to experiment with different approaches. One of the best ways to reach people is by developing need-meeting ministries for specific groups. One pastor used to say, "Meet people at their point of need or pain and you'll have no shortage of people."[3] Social networks empower evangelism among groups of people who have common interests or affinities. One obvious social network is friends and family members. Others include special interest groups, like mountain bike riders (or Harley riders), book lovers, musicians, racquetball players, gardeners, landscape painters, and a host of others.

Invite Faith in Christ

Remember that the purpose of all these activities is to give people the opportunity to believe in Jesus Christ alone for their salvation. A clear theme of Scripture is the challenge to repent and believe on Jesus Christ. Of course our challenges to people must be tempered with sensitivity and common sense, particularly among resistant populations. Nevertheless, some opportunity for people to affirm their belief should always be offered. Much of the time, in the effort to build relationships, we forget to ask our unbelieving friends, family, and associates to put their faith in Christ. The claims of Christianity demand a verdict, a decision for or against Jesus Christ. Your church must be intentional in giving people the opportunity to make that commitment.

One of the dangers in serving people is forgetting to tell them about their sinfulness; the death, burial, and resurrection of Jesus, which provides for their forgiveness; and the need to make a decision to accept Jesus as their Savior. We must love, serve, and care for those outside of Jesus Christ, but the best way to love them, serve them, and care for them is to help them make a personal faith commitment to him. Perhaps the reason your church is not seeing more people come to faith in Christ is that you are not asking them to make a faith decision. Our goal is to make lifelong disciples, and discipleship always begins with a decision!

Look in the Mirror

Once or twice a year a church needs to look in the mirror. We need to take a critical look at our church facility, our services, and our ministries to determine how they appear to people outside the church. Is the facility inviting? Are our services interesting and do they inspire worship? Do our ministries meet real needs?

You may want to hire someone, preferably an unbeliever, to be a secret guest. Ask the person to visit your church's worship service or services and then provide feedback on what they found. To gain different perspectives, hire a man one time and a woman another time. Then ask a family to come and evaluate the children's ministry or youth program. Hire a younger, middle-aged, or older couple to attend activities and share what they observed. Ask an unchurched person to evaluate your church's website. Since younger people often connect initially with a church's website, it is best if the evaluator is under thirty years old. Ask them to tell you what is missing, difficult to understand, working or not working on the site, and what they recommend to improve it.

Encourage Involvement in the Community

Encourage the people who are currently attending the church to be involved in the community. Survey worshipers to determine the percentage of people connected to community groups, as well as the types of groups in which they serve. This will give you insight into what programs or ministries your church might offer that could meet the interests and needs of unchurched people and families. People in your church can be involved in a wide range of community activities where they can do incarnational evangelism. They could choose, for example, to work with Habitat for Humanity, coach children's sports, join a service club (such as Kiwanis), participate in political action groups, or get involved in numerous other arenas of service.

Have a Strategy

It is important that your church develop a strategy for connecting new believers with members of the church and getting them involved in ministry and small groups. One of the weaknesses of evangelistic churches is the neglect of follow-up.

First there must be a plan for welcoming and connecting with guests when they first come to the church. The strategy for greeting guests should include the opportunities presented at each of the following points of contact:

- As people drive into your church parking lot
- As people exit their cars in the parking lot
- While people are walking to the church from the parking lot
- Before people enter the church building
- As people enter the church building
- As people look for help with children or other services
- When people enter the worship auditorium/sanctuary
- During the worship service
- When people exit the worship service, pick up their children, and leave the building

It is also important to design a plan to connect with these guests in the weeks to come. Think through a strategy for following up with guests the week after their first, second, third, and fourth visits to your church. Not only is this biblical but it helps the new believer to affirm his or her decision to believe in Christ and come to your church. New believers always second-guess or reevaluate their decision to follow Christ. If they are not connected to a local church, there is a strong possibility they will drift away from their newfound faith.

Remain Humble

The process of salvation is ultimately in God's control. We must appreciate the profound nature of spiritual transformation and growth. Recognizing that "our adequacy is from God" (2 Cor. 3:5), we must continue in prayer, trusting God to bring about spiritual fruit in his time. Planning for evangelism must be rooted in faith, perseverance, prayer, and patience. Faith and prayer enable us to trust God with the results, while perseverance and patience allow us to keep doing our part of proclaiming the message of salvation.

Does the King of Kings Still Care about the Lost?

Following his call to ministry by Jesus, Matthew (Levi) "gave a big reception for Him in his house; and there was a great crowd of tax collectors and other people who were reclining at the table with them" (Luke 5:29). The Pharisees complained that Jesus ate and drank with sinners. Jesus responded by explaining his mission, "I have not come to call the righteous but sinners to repentance" (v. 32). The fact that he spent a lot of time with lost sinners is echoed in Jesus's commenting on the Pharisees' complaints that he was "a gluttonous man and a drunkard, a friend of tax collectors and sinners!" (7:34). His emphasis on sinners finding repentance became a dominant theme in the rest of the Gospel of Luke.

The ministry of Jesus was characterized by radical love for those on the margins of society. He especially made a priority of ministering to women, Samaritans, Gentiles, the sick, the poor, and the disliked. Typically his ministry included acts of healing and care, but it is clear that he passed by many sick, poor, and disadvantaged without serving them directly. His promise of salvation to sinners was the distinctive characteristic of his message. He said he had "come to seek and to save that which was lost" (19:10).

The question for us is this: Does Jesus, the King of Kings, still care about the lost? The answer most assuredly is *yes.* He does still care. He cared about me, he cared about you, and he continues to care for all those who remain separated from him by their sin. "For God so loved the world, that He gave His only begotten Son, that whoever believes in Him shall not perish, but have eternal life" (John 3:16). He stands ready to accept and redeem those who believe in him alone for their salvation. "He who believes in Him is not judged" (v. 18). As he said, "Come to Me, all who are weary and heavy-laden, and I will give you rest. . . . and you will find rest for your souls" (Matt. 11:28–29).

A more personal question is this: Do we and our church still care about the lost? Are we inviting others to dine with Jesus? One thing that seems to be clear, both from the Bible and research, is that unbelievers are brought to Christ primarily when they engage in spiritual conversations with family members and friends. God can win people to faith in Jesus Christ without our participation, but he rarely does so, preferring in his sovereignty to work through us, his people, to proclaim the gospel of salvation to lost men and women, boys and girls. May we have the courage to love the lost as much as Jesus Christ and to engage in proclaiming the gospel until he comes in all his glory. Let's get started inviting others to dine with Jesus!

Probing Questions

1. Which of the ideas in this chapter for inviting others to dine with Jesus are you already doing?
2. Which ideas are you ignoring or missing in your evangelism strategy?
3. What are you going to do this year to start to or better engage in inviting people to dine with Jesus?

Appendix

Survey Instrument

1. What *person* was it that led you to come to *faith in Christ*?
   - ☐ Member of the pastoral staff
   - ☐ Family member
   - ☐ Neighbor
   - ☐ Colleague at work
   - ☐ Friend
   - ☐ Other (please specify): _____

2. What *method* most influenced your desire to come to *faith in Christ*? (Mark only one.)
   - ☐ A visit by someone from the church staff
   - ☐ A conversation with a family member
   - ☐ A conversation with a friend/neighbor
   - ☐ A conversation with a colleague from work
   - ☐ Attended a large crusade or other special event

☐ Special need (please specify): _____

☐ Other (please specify): _____

3. What person was the greatest influence in your attending this church? (Mark only one.)

☐ Neighbor

☐ Friend

☐ Co-worker

☐ Merchant

☐ Family member

☐ No one

☐ Other (please specify)_____

4. Were the *theological beliefs* of the church important in your decision to attend this church?

☐ Yes

☐ No

☐ Uncertain

5. Was the friendliness of the church a major factor in your decision to join your church?

☐ Yes

☐ No

☐ Uncertain

6. Did the location of the church influence your decision to attend?

☐ Yes

☐ No

☐ Somewhat

7. Did the name of the church influence your decision to join?

    ☐ Yes

    ☐ No

    ☐ Uncertain

8. Did the pastor's preaching play a part in your coming to church?

    ☐ Yes

    ☐ No

    ☐ Uncertain

9. Before attending this church, did you regularly attend a church somewhere else?

    ☐ Yes

    ☐ No

10. If you answered "yes" to question 9, *why* did you leave your previous church? (Mark only one.)

    ☐ Job relocation

    ☐ Moved away

    ☐ Problems at previous church

    ☐ Desire for different type/style of church

    ☐ Other (please specify)_____

11. If you answered "no" to question 9, *how long* had it been since you attended a church on a regular basis?

    ☐ I never attended a church before

    ☐ Less than two years

    ☐ 3–5 years

    ☐ 6–10 years

☐ 11–15 years

☐ 16–20 years

☐ over 20 years

12. How many times in a year did you visit a church (for any service) when you had no church affiliation?

☐ 0 times

☐ 1 time

☐ 2 times

☐ 3 times

☐ More than 3 times

☐ Does not apply

13. If applicable, which family member influenced your coming to church? (Mark only one.)

☐ It was not a family member

☐ Spouse

☐ Sibling(s)

☐ Child(ren)

☐ Parent(s)

☐ In-law(s)

☐ Other (please specify): _____

14. What factors of the pastor's ministry influenced your choice of this church? (Check no more than three.)

☐ Preaching that teaches and applies to my life

☐ Authenticity of the pastor

☐ Pastor's conviction

☐ Pastor's leadership skills

☐ Personal contact by the pastor

☐ Feeling at ease when around the pastor

☐ Pastor's sense of humor

☐ A class led by the pastor

☐ Other (please specify): _____

15. Rank in order the *reasons* why you chose to attend your current church. Use 1 for the most important reason and 14 for the least important reason. Don't use the same number twice.

____The preaching of the pastor

____The style of the music/worship program

____The church's theological position

____A family member attends here

____Age-group programs (children's, youth, singles, etc.)

____Proximity to where I live

____I was invited by a neighbor/friend

____Small group

____Church website

____Christian day school/preschool

____A recovery ministry program (divorce, grief, etc.)

____Sunday school/church school

____Just happened to drive by the church

____Other (please specify):_____

16. Which of the following influenced your desire to stay at the church? (Check all that apply.)

☐ I gained a clearer understanding of Christian beliefs and teachings

☐ The church had low expectations of me as a newcomer

☐ The church had high expectations of me as a newcomer

☐ The church had a new members class

☐ The style of worship in the service

☐ The church had small groups

☐ The church had Sunday school/church school

☐ The church had a clear mission and vision

☐ The church had a place for me to serve

☐ Other (please specify): _____

17. What were your first impressions when you first visited this church?

_____

18. What were your impressions on subsequent visits?

_____

19. Does your church require you to attend an orientation class before becoming a member?

☐ Attending a new members class is required for membership

☐ Attending a new members class is expected but not required

☐ Attending a new members class is offered but not expected

☐ Our church does not offer formal membership

☐ Uncertain

20. Do you regularly attend any of the following programs at your church? (Check all that apply.)

☐ Sunday school

☐ Bible studies

☐ Small group

☐ Other (please specify): _____

☐ I do not regularly attend a weekly function at my church (excluding worship services)

21. Gender

    ☐ Male   ☐ Female

22. What generation do you belong to?

    ☐ Builders (born before 1945)

    ☐ Baby Boomers (born between 1946 and 1964)

    ☐ Generation X (born between 1965 and 1984)

    ☐ Millennials (born after 1984)

23. Do you attend a Sunday school class on a regular basis?

    ☐ Yes   ☐ No

    If yes, please explain your primary motivation for attending: _____

    If no, please explain your reason(s) for not attending:

    _____

24. How important is religious faith in your life?

    ☐ Not important   ☐ Fairly important

    ☐ Slightly important   ☐ Very important

25. How many miles do you live from your church?

    ☐ 0–1 mile

    ☐ 2–5 miles

    ☐ 6–10 miles

    ☐ 11–20 miles

    ☐ 21–30 miles

    ☐ More than 30 miles

26. What size city do you live in?
    - ☐ Metropolis (population: 1 million+)
    - ☐ Large city (population: 500,000–1 million)
    - ☐ Medium city (population: 100,000–500,000)
    - ☐ Small city (population : 25,000–100,000)
    - ☐ Small town (population : 10,000–25,000)
    - ☐ Rural (population less than 10,000)

27. What is your church affiliation?
    - ☐ Assemblies of God
    - ☐ Baptist
    - ☐ Catholic
    - ☐ Episcopalian
    - ☐ Free Church traditions
    - ☐ Lutheran
    - ☐ Methodist
    - ☐ Presbyterian
    - ☐ Nondenominational
    - ☐ Other (please specify): _____

28. Are you currently involved in a ministry at your church?
    ☐ Yes   ☐ No
    If yes, please identify it:_____

29. What is the greatest personal benefit you receive from attending this church?

    _____

    _____

    _____

Notes

Chapter 2 What Is Our Mission?

1. *Doxology* means giving praise or glory to God.

2. Several missions (plural) for Jesus Christ are mentioned by biblical scholars; for example, his mission as Creator, his mission as Sustainer, and his mission as Messiah.

3. The word *life* is used thirty-six times in the Gospel of John—eleven of them with the adjective *eternal*.

Chapter 3 What Is Our Priority?

1. Craig Van Gelder, *The Essence of the Church* (Grand Rapids: Baker, 2000), 125.

2. Kenneth Scott Latourette, *A History of the Expansion of Christianity: The First Five Centuries* (New York: Harper and Brothers, 1937), 1:186.

3. Other references to "good news" are found in Isaiah 40:9; 41:27; 60:6; and 61:1.

4. Alan R. Tippett, *The Jesus Documents*, ed. Shawn Redford and Doug Priest (Pasadena, CA: William Carey Library, 2012), 44.

5. For an extended discussion of the lexical, contextual, and corroborative data on the meaning of "poor," see David J. Hesselgrave, *Paradigms in Conflict* (Grand Rapids: Kregel, 2005), 125–35.

6. Arthur F. Glasser et al., *Announcing the Kingdom* (Grand Rapids: Baker, 2003), 358.

7. Tippett, *The Jesus Documents*, 46.

8. Ibid., 47.

9. Some see Luke 4:18–19 as Jesus's mission statement. See James Engel and William Dyrness, *Changing the Mind of Missions: Where Have We Gone Wrong?*

(Downers Grove, IL: InterVarsity, 2000), 23. However, Luke 19:10 seems a better choice as his mission statement.

10. See, for example, the work of the Gates Foundation and of the Acumen Fund, among others.

Chapter 4 What Is Our Role?

1. Mark used the word *disciple* forty-six times from the second chapter on throughout the book. The word *apostles*, as found in Mark 6:30, was used of disciples.

2. The words *straightway* and *immediately*, from the Greek *eutheos*, occur more than thirty times throughout the book of Mark. It was one of the features of Mark that Jesus came not only preaching but also healing with great power, i.e., he took action to change things.

3. A. T. Robertson, *Matthew and Mark*, Word Pictures in the New Testament (Nashville: Broadman, 1930), 251.

4. Tippett, *Jesus Documents,* 34.

5. W. Robert Cook, "God's Decree and the Work of Evangelism" (unpublished manuscript, Western Conservative Baptist Seminary, c. 1971), 6.

6. Ibid., 6.

Chapter 5 What Is Our Focus?

1. A. R. Tippett, *Verdict Theology in Missionary Theory* (Pasadena, CA: William Carey Library, 1973), 150.

Chapter 6 What Is Our Context?

1. John F. Walvoord, *The Prophecy Knowledge Handbook: All the Prophecies of Scripture Explained in One Volume* (Wheaton: Victor, 1990), 369–71.

2. This is true as long as the churches, associations, and denominations are biblically orthodox. While each church group has its own theological perspectives and identity, it is generally agreed that it is most important for people to believe by faith in Jesus Christ for their salvation.

Chapter 7 Who Led You to Faith in Christ?

1. Donald Anderson McGavran, *The Bridges of God* (London: World Dominion Press, 1955), 4; distributed in the United States by Friendship Press, New York.

2. This question violated one of the principles of writing a questionnaire, that is, a question should just ask one question. This question asks two, which makes it difficult to know exactly which of the two the respondent is answering.

3. Win Arn and Charles Arn, *The Master's Plan for Making Disciples* (1982; repr., Pasadena, CA: Church Growth Press, 1998).

4. Institute for American Church Growth, "Background of the Master's Plan" (unpublished report, c. 1982).

5. See "Design of the Study" in chapter 1 for a full description.

6. Dr. Gordon Penfold is director of FreshStart and can be reached at gordon pnfld@gmail.com.

Chapter 10 Why Do You Remain at Your Church?

1. Chuck Lawless, *Membership Matters: Insights from Effective Churches on New Member Classes and Assimilation* (Grand Rapids: Zondervan, 2005).

Chapter 11 What Is the Pastor's Role in Evangelism?

1. Gary L. McIntosh and Charles Arn, *What Every Pastor Should Know: 101 Indispensable Rules of Thumb for Leading Your Church* (Grand Rapids: Baker, 2013), 26.

Chapter 12 Principles of Effective Evangelism

1. McIntosh and Arn, *What Every Pastor Should Know*, 25–26.

Chapter 13 Inviting Others to Dine with Jesus

1. Some prepackaged training programs that churches have used effectively include *Outflow, Becoming a Contagious Christian,* and *Just Walk across the Room.* For information on these, check the internet or email the author.

2. For practical ideas on starting events, see McIntosh and Arn, *What Every Pastor Should Know,* 19–22.

3. Dale Galloway, "Ten Characteristics of a Healthy Church," *Net Results,* May 1998.

Services Available

Gary L. McIntosh speaks to numerous churches, nonprofit organizations, schools, and conventions each year. Services available include keynote presentations at major meetings, seminars and workshops, training courses, and ongoing consultation.

For a live presentation of the material found in *Growing God's Church* or to request information on Dr. McIntosh's availability and ministry, contact:

Church Growth Network
PO Box 892589
Temecula, CA 92589-2589
951/506-3086
Twitter: @drgmcintosh
Email: cgnet@earthlink.net
World Wide Web: www.churchgrowthnetwork.com

Gary L. McIntosh is a nationally and internationally known speaker, writer, and professor of Christian ministry and leadership. He is recognized as the foremost spokesperson for classical church growth missiology in the United States. As a church growth expert, he publishes *Growth Points,* a monthly publication read by more than seven thousand church leaders. Dr. McIntosh is in wide demand as a speaker and seminar leader on numerous subjects related to church life and ministry. He has published more than three hundred articles and reviews in Christian magazines and journals and is the author of twenty-four books including *One Size Doesn't Fit All*; *One Church, Four Generations*; *Staff Your Church for Growth*; *Biblical Church Growth*; and the award-winning *What Every Pastor Should Know: 101 Indispensable Rules of Thumb for Leading Your Church* (with Charles Arn, Baker Books, 2013).

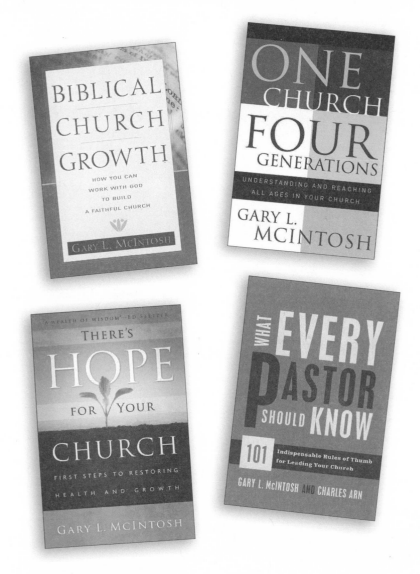